HARCOURT SCIENCE
ASSESSMENT GUIDE

Harcourt School Publishers

Orlando • Boston • Dallas • Chicago • San Diego

www.harcourtschool.com

Copyright © by Harcourt, Inc.

All rights reserved. No part of this publication may be reproduced or transmitted in any form or by any means, electronic or mechanical, including photocopy, recording, or any information storage and retrieval system, without permission in writing from the publisher.

Permission is hereby granted to individual teachers using the corresponding student's textbook or kit as the major vehicle for regular classroom instruction to photocopy Copying Masters from this publication in classroom quantities for instructional use and not for resale. Requests for information on other matters regarding duplication of this work should be addressed to School Permissions and Copyrights, Harcourt, Inc., 6277 Sea Harbor Drive, Orlando, Florida 32887-6777. Fax: 407-345-2418.

HARCOURT and the Harcourt Logo are trademarks of Harcourt, Inc., registered in the United States of America and/or jurisdictions.

Printed in the United States of America

ISBN 0-15-323705-8

7 8 9 10 054 10 09 08 07 06 05 04

Contents

Overview .... AGv
Assessment Components .... AGvi
Formal Assessment .... AGvii
Test-Taking Tips .... AGviii
Performance Assessment .... AGix
Scoring a Performance Task .... AGxi
Classroom Observation .... AGxii
Observation Checklist .... AGxiv
Using Student Self-Assessment .... AGxv
Self-Assessment—Investigate .... AGxvi
Self-Assessment—Learn About .... AGxvii
Experiment/Project Evaluation Checklist .... AGxviii
Experiment/Project Summary Sheet .... AGxix
Portfolio Assessment .... AGxx
Science Experiences Record .... AGxxii
Guide to My Science Portfolio .... AGxxiii
Portfolio Evaluation Checklist .... AGxxiv

UNIT A — Plants and Animals All Around

Chapter 1—Living and Nonliving Things AG1
Performance Task AG5
Chapter 2—All About Plants AG7
Performance Task AG11
Chapter 3—All About Animals AG13
Performance Task AG17
Unit A Test AG19

UNIT B — Living Together

Chapter 1—Plants and Animals Need One Another AG23
Performance Task AG27
Chapter 2—A Place to Live AG29
Performance Task AG33
Unit B Test AG35

UNIT C — About Our Earth

Chapter 1—Earth's Land AG39
Performance Task AG43
Chapter 2—Our Natural Resources AG45
Performance Task AG49
Unit C Test AG51

UNIT D — Weather, the Sky, and Seasons

Chapter 1—Measuring Weather AG55
Performance Task AG59
Chapter 2—The Sky and the Seasons AG61
Performance Task AG65
Unit D Test AG67

UNIT E — Matter and Energy

Chapter 1—Investigate Matter AG71
Performance Task AG75
Chapter 2—Making Sound AG77
Performance Task AG81
Unit E Test AG83

UNIT F — Forces

Chapter 1—Pushes and Pulls AG87
Performance Task AG91
Chapter 2—Magnets AG93
Performance Task AG97
Unit F Test AG99

Answer Key AG103–AG121

Overview

In *Harcourt Science,* the Assessment Program, like the instruction, is student-centered. By allowing all learners to show what they know and can do, the program provides you with ongoing information about each student's understanding of science. Equally important, the Assessment Program involves the student in self-evaluation, offering you strategies for helping students evaluate their own growth.

The *Harcourt Science* Assessment Program is based on the Assessment Model in the chart below. The model's framework shows the multidimensional aspect of the program, with five kinds of assessment, supported by both teacher-based and student-based assessment tools.

The teacher-based strand, the left column in the model, involves assessments in which the teacher evaluates a student product as evidence of the student's understanding of chapter content and of his or her ability to think critically about it. The teacher-based strand consists of two components: Formal Assessment and Performance Assessment.

The student-based strand, the right column in the model, involves assessments that invite the student to become a partner in the assessment process. These student-based assessments encourage students to reflect on and evaluate their own efforts. The student-based strand also consists of two components: Student Self-Assessment and Portfolio Assessment.

There is a fifth component in the *Harcourt Science* assessment program—Ongoing Assessment, which involves classroom observation and informal evaluation of students' growth in science knowledge and process skills. This essential component is listed in the center of the Assessment Model because it is the "glue" that binds together all the other types of assessment.

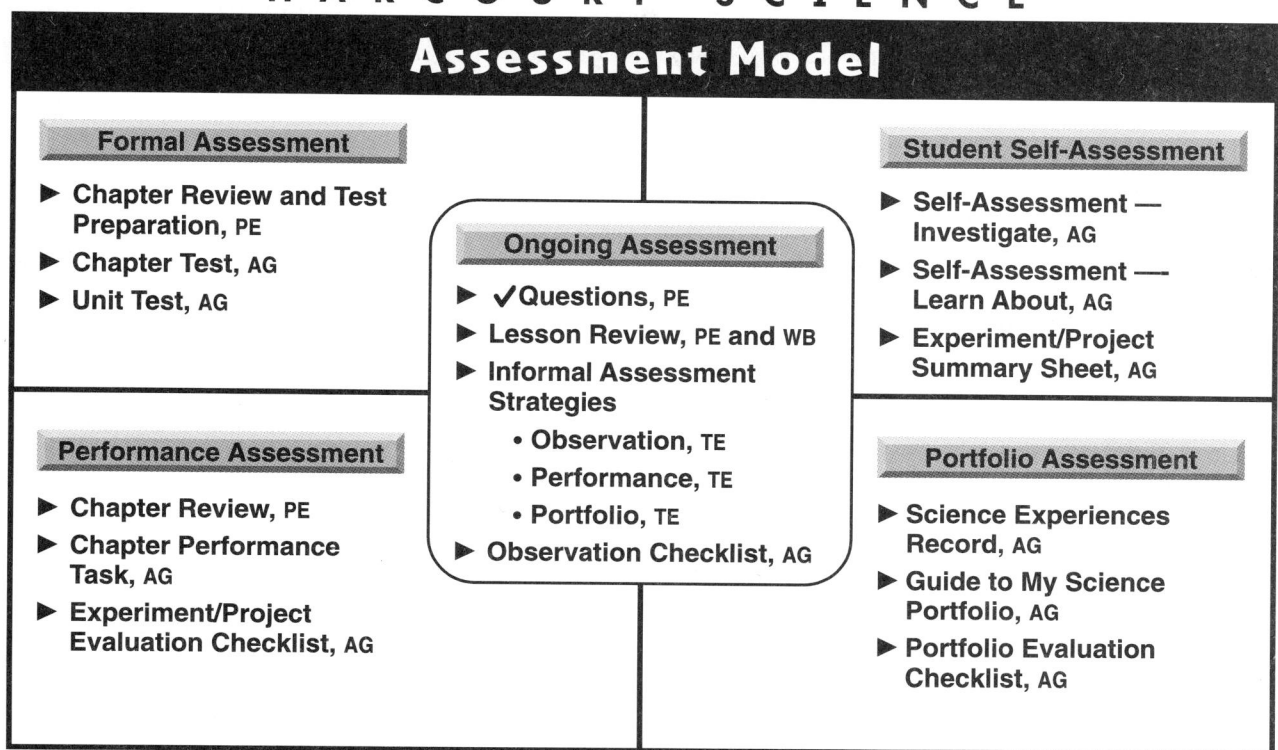

(**Key:** PE=Pupil Edition; TE=Teacher's Edition; AG=Assessment Guide; WB=Workbook)

Assessment Components

Formal Assessment

Research into the learning process has shown the positive effects of periodic review. To help you reinforce and assess mastery of chapter objectives, *Harcourt Science* includes both reviews and tests. You will find the Chapter Review and Test Preparation in the pupil book and the Chapter Test and Unit Test in this **Assessment Guide.** Answers to all assessments, including sample responses to open-ended items, are provided.

Performance Assessment

Science literacy involves not only what students know but also how they think and how they do things. Performance tasks provide evidence of students' ability to use science process skills and critical thinking skills to complete an authentic problem-solving task. A performance task is included in each chapter review. Another follows each Chapter Test in this **Assessment Guide.** Each includes teacher directions and a scoring rubric. Also in this booklet, you will find the Experiment/Project Evaluation Checklist (p. AGxviii), for evaluating unit experiments and projects.

Ongoing Assessment

Opportunities abound for observing and evaluating student growth during regular classroom instruction in science. *Harcourt Science* supports this informal, ongoing assessment in several ways: Within each lesson in the **Pupil Edition** (grades 3–6), there are boldface ✔ questions at the end of sections to help you assess students' immediate recall of information. Then, at the end of each lesson, there is a Lesson Review to help you evaluate how well students grasped the concepts taught. The Lesson Review also includes a multiple-choice "test prep" question. In grades 1 and 2, caption questions and Think About It after every lesson are tools for ongoing assessment. Additional material for reviewing the lesson is provided in the **Workbook.**

The **Teacher's Edition** offers Informal Assessment Strategies. These strategies, which appear at point of use within chapters, give ideas for integrating classroom observation, performance assessment, and portfolio assessment with instruction. Located in this **Assessment Guide** is yet another tool, the Observation Checklist (pp. AGxiv), on which you can record noteworthy classroom observations.

Student Self-Assessment

Self-assessment can have significant and positive effects on student achievement. To achieve these effects, students must be challenged to reflect on their work and to monitor, analyze, and control their own learning. Located in this **Assessment Guide** are two checklists designed to do just that. One is Self-Assessment—Investigate (p. AGxvi), which leads students to assess their performance and growth in science skills after completing Investigate in the **Pupil Edition.** The second is Self-Assessment— Learn About (p. AGxvii), a checklist to help the student reflect on instruction in a particular lesson or chapter in *Harcourt Science*. Also in this booklet, following the checklists, you will find the Experiment/Project Summary Sheet (p. AGxix), on which students describe and evaluate their own science projects and experiments.

Portfolio Assessment

In *Harcourt Science*, students may create their own portfolios. The portfolio holds self-selected work samples that the student feels represent gains in his or her understanding of science concepts and use of science processes. The portfolio may also contain a few required or teacher-selected papers. Support materials are included in this **Assessment Guide** (pp. AGxx–AGxxiv) to assist you and your students in developing portfolios and in using them to evaluate growth in science skills.

Formal Assessment

Formal assessment is an essential part of any comprehensive assessment program because it provides an objective measure of student achievement. This traditional form of assessment typically consists of reviews and tests that assess how well students understand, communicate, and apply what they have learned. This is the type of assessment that is typically used in state and local standardized tests in science.

Formal Assessment in *Harcourt Science*

Formal assessment in the *Harcourt Science* program includes the following measures: Chapter Review in **Pupil Edition** grades 1 and 2; Chapter Review and Test Preparation in **Pupil Edition** grades 3–6; and Chapter and Unit Assessments in this **Assessment Guide.** The purpose of the review is to assess and reinforce not only chapter concepts and science skills but also students' test-taking skills. The purpose of the Chapter and Unit Assessments is, as with other formal assessments, to provide an objective measure of student performance. Answers to chapter reviews, including sample responses to open-ended items, are located in the Teacher's Edition, while answers to chapter and unit tests are located in the Answer Key in this booklet.

Types of Review and Test Items

Students can be overwhelmed by the amount of information on a test and uneasy about how to answer different types of test questions about this information. The Chapter Review and Test Preparation is designed to help familiarize students with the various item formats they may encounter: *multiple-choice items* (with a question stem; sentence fragment; graph, table, map, model, or picture; or using negatives such as *not, least,* and so on), *open-ended items* (which require the student to write a short answer, to record data, or to order items), and *scenarios,* in which the student is asked to respond to several items in either a multiple-choice or open-ended format.

Test-Taking Tips

Harcourt Science offers test-taking tips—aimed at improving student performance on formal assessment—in the Teacher's Edition. The section titled Test Prep—Test-Taking Tips spells out what students can do to analyze and interpret multiple-choice or open-ended types of questions. Each tip suggests a strategy that students can use to help them come up with the correct answer to an item. Included in the strategies are tips to help students

- focus on the question.
- understand unfamiliar words.
- identify key information.
- analyze and interpret graphs, charts, and tables.
- eliminate incorrect answer choices.
- find the correct answer.
- mark the correct answer.

The tips include the following suggestions:

- Scan the entire test first before answering any questions.
- Read the directions slowly and carefully before you begin a section.
- Begin with the easiest questions or most familiar material.
- Read the question and *all* answer options before selecting an answer.
- Watch out for key words such as *not*, *least*, and so on.
- Double-check answers to catch and correct errors.
- Erase all mistakes completely and write corrections neatly.

Test Preparation

Students perform better on formal assessments when they are well prepared for the testing situation. Here are some things you can do before a test to help your students do their best work.

- Explain the nature of the test to students.
- Suggest that they review the questions at the end of the lessons and the chapter.
- Remind students to get a good night's sleep before the test.
- Discuss why they should eat a balanced meal beforehand.
- Encourage students to relax while they take the test.

Performance Assessment

Teachers today have come to realize that the multiple-choice format of traditional tests, while useful and efficient, cannot provide a complete picture of students' growth in science. Standardized tests may show what students know, but they are not designed to show how they *think and do things*—an essential aspect of science literacy. Performance assessment, along with other types of assessments, can supply the missing information and help balance your assessment program.

An important feature of performance assessment is that it involves a hands-on activity to solve a situational problem. An advantage of this type of assessment is that students often find it more enjoyable than the traditional paper-and-pencil test. Another advantage is that it models good instruction: students are assessed as they learn and learn as they are assessed.

Performance Assessment in *Harcourt Science*

The performance task, science project, unit experiment, and other hands-on science activities provide good opportunities for performance assessment. The performance task is particularly useful because it provides insights into the student's ability to apply key science process skills and concepts taught in the chapter.

At grades 3–6, *Harcourt Science* provides performance assessment in the Chapter Review and Test Preparation feature in the pupil book and in the Chapter Test in this **Assessment Guide**. In the review at grades 1 and 2, the performance assessment is the last item of the Chapter Review; in the test, it is a performance task. The Experiment/Project Evaluation Checklist (p. AGxviii) is a measure you can use to evaluate unit experiments and projects.

Administering Performance Tasks

Unlike traditional assessment tools, performance assessment does not provide standardized directions for its administration or impose specific time limits on students, although a time frame is suggested as a guideline. The suggestions that follow may help you define your role in this assessment.

▶ *Be prepared.*

A few days before students begin the task, read the Teacher's Directions and gather the materials needed.

▶ *Be clear.*

Explain the directions for the task; rephrase them as needed. Also, explain how students' performance will be evaluated. Present the rubric you plan to use and explain the performance indicators in language your students understand.

▶ *Be encouraging.*

Your role in administering the assessments should be that of a coach—motivating, guiding, and encouraging students to produce their best work.

▶ *Be supportive.*

You may assist students who need help. The amount of assistance needed will depend on the needs and abilities of individual students.

▶ *Be flexible.*

All students need not proceed through the performance task at the same rate and in the same manner. Allow them adequate time to do their best work.

▶ *Involve students in evaluation.*

Invite students to join you as partners in the evaluation process, particularly in development or modification of the rubric.

Rubrics for Assessing Performance

A well-written rubric can help you score students' work accurately and fairly. Moreover, it gives students a better idea of what qualities their work should exhibit *before* they begin a task.

Each performance task in the program has its own rubric. The rubric lists performance indicators, which are brief statements of what to look for in assessing the skills and understandings that the task addresses. A sample rubric follows.

Scoring Rubric

Performance Indicators

_____ Assembles the kite successfully.

_____ Carries out the experiment daily.

_____ Records results accurately.

_____ Makes an accurate chart and uses it to report the strength of wind observed each day.

Performance Indicators

| 3 | 2 | 1 | 0 |

Scoring a Performance Task

The scoring system used for program performance tasks is a 4-point scale (3-2-1-0) that is compatible with those used by many state assessment programs. You may wish to modify the rubrics as a 3- or 5-point scale, as your individual needs and circumstances require. To determine a student's score on a performance task, review the indicators checked on the rubric and then select the score that best represents the student's overall performance on the task.

4-Point Scale			
Excellent Achievement	Adequate Achievement	Limited Achievement	Little or No Achievement
3	2	1	0

How to Convert a Rubric Score into a Grade

If, for grading purposes, you want to record a letter or numerical grade rather than a holistic score for the student's performance on a task, you can use the following conversion table:

Holistic Score	Letter Grade	Numerical Grade
3	A	90–100
2	B	80–89
1	C	70–79
0	D–F	69 or below

Developing Your Own Rubric

From time to time, you may want to either develop your own rubric or work together with your students to create one. Research has shown that significantly improved performance can result from student participation in the construction of rubrics.

Developing a rubric for a performance task involves three basic steps: (1) Identify the process skills taught in the chapter that students must perform to complete the task successfully and identify what understanding of content is also required. (2) Determine which skill/understanding is involved in each step. (3) Decide what you will look for to confirm that the student has acquired each skill and understanding you identified.

Classroom Observation

"Kid watching" is a natural part of teaching and an important part of evaluation. The purpose of classroom observation in assessment is to gather and record information that can lead to improved instruction. In this booklet, you will find an Observation Checklist (p. AGxiv) on which you can record noteworthy observations of students' ability to use science process skills.

Using the Observation Checklist

▶ *Identify the skills you will observe.*
Find out which science process skills are introduced and reinforced in the chapter.

▶ *Focus on only a few students at a time.*
You will find this more effective than trying to observe the entire class at once.

▶ *Look for a pattern.*
It is important to observe the student's strengths and weaknesses over a period of time to determine whether a pattern exists.

▶ *Plan how and when to record observations.*
Decide whether to
- record observations immediately on the checklist as you move about the room or
- make jottings or mental notes of observations and record them later.

▶ *Don't agonize over the ratings.*
Students who stand out as particularly strong will clearly merit a rating of *3* ("Outstanding"). Others may clearly earn a rating of *1* ("Needs Improvement"). This doesn't mean, however, that a *2* ("Satisfactory") is automatically the appropriate rating for the rest of the class. For example, you may not have had sufficient opportunity to observe a student demonstrate certain skills. The checklist cells for these skills should remain blank under the student's name until you have observed him or her perform the skills.

▶ *Review your checklist periodically and ask yourself questions such as:*

What are the student's strongest/weakest attributes?

In what ways has the student shown growth?

In what areas does the class as a whole show strength/weakness?

What kinds of activities would encourage growth?

Do I need to allot more time to classroom observation?

▶ **Use the data you collect.**

Refer to your classroom observation checklists when you plan lessons, form groups, assign grades, and confer with students and family members.

Date _____

Observation Checklist

Rating Scale	
3 Outstanding	**1** Needs Improvement
2 Satisfactory	☐ Not Enough Opportunity to Observe

Names of Students

Science Process Skills											
Observe											
Compare											
Classify/Order											
Gather, Record, Display, or Interpret Data											
Use Numbers											
Communicate											
Plan and Conduct Simple Investigations											
Measure											
Predict											
Infer											
Draw Conclusions											
Use Time/Space Relationships											
Hypothesize											
Formulate or Use Models											
Identify and Control Variables											
Experiment											

AG xiv Assessment Guide **Grade 1**

Using Student Self-Assessment

Researchers have evidence that self-evaluation and the reflection it involves can have positive effects on students' learning. To achieve these effects, students must be challenged to reflect on their work and to monitor, analyze, and control their own learning—beginning in the earliest grades.

Frequent opportunities for students to evaluate their performance builds the skills and confidence they need for effective self-assessment. A trusting relationship between the student and the teacher is also essential. Students must be assured that honest responses can have only a positive effect on the teacher's view of them, and that they will not be used to determine grades.

Student Self-Assessment in *Harcourt Science*

The assessment program offers three self-assessment measures, which are located in this booklet. The first one is Self-Assessment—Investigate: a form that invites students to reflect on how they felt about, and what they learned from, Investigate, a hands-on investigation at the beginning of each lesson. The second measure is Self-Assessment—Learn About: a form that leads students to reflect on and evaluate what they learned from reading and instruction in Learn About at either the lesson or chapter level. The third is the Experiment/Project Summary Sheet—a form to help students describe and evaluate their unit experiments and projects.

Using Self-Assessment Forms

▶ *Explain the directions.*
Discuss the forms and how to complete them.

▶ *Encourage honest responses.*
Be sure to tell students that there are no "right" responses to the items.

▶ *Model the process.*
One way to foster candid responses is to model the process yourself, including at least one response that is not positive. Discuss reasons for your responses.

▶ *Be open to variations in students' responses.*
Negative responses should not be viewed as indicating weaknesses. Rather they confirm that you did a good job of communicating the importance of honesty in self-assessment.

▶ *Discuss responses with students.*
You may wish to clarify students' responses in conferences with them and in family conferences. Invite both students and family members to help you plan activities for school and home that will motivate and support their growth in science.

Name _____
Date _____

Self-Assessment—Investigate

How Did I Do?

Investigate was about _____
_____

How did you do? Circle the word that tells what you think. If you are not sure, circle the **?**.

1. I followed the directions. **Yes ? No**
2. I worked well with others. **Yes ? No**
3. I was careful with materials. **Yes ? No**
4. I completed the investigation. **Yes ? No**
5. The science skill that I learned was

[   ]

6. I found out _____
_____
_____
_____

AG xvi Assessment Guide   Grade 1

Name _____
Lesson _____

Self-Assessment— Learn About

Think Back!

How did you do? Circle the word that tells what you think. If you are not sure, circle the **?**.

1. I could read the lesson.   **Yes ? No**
2. I used the pictures to help me read.   **Yes ? No**
3. I answered the questions by the pictures.   **Yes ? No**
4. I asked questions when I did not understand something.   **Yes ? No**
5. I understood most of the ideas.   **Yes ? No**
6. I could answer most of the questions in Think About It.   **Yes ? No**

This is something I learned.
_____
_____

I learned these new words.
_____
_____

Grade 1

Assessment Guide AG xvii

Name _____

Date _____

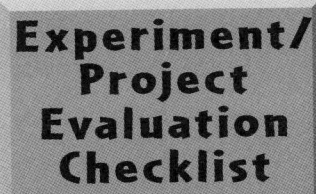

Experiment/Project Evaluation

Aspects of Science Literacy	Evidence of Growth
1. **Understands science concepts** (Animals, Plants; Earth's Land, Air, Water, Space; Weather; Matter, Motion, Energy)	
2. **Uses science process skills** (observes, compares, classifies, gathers/interprets data, communicates, measures, experiments, infers, predicts, draws conclusions)	
3. **Thinks critically** (analyzes, synthesizes, evaluates, applies ideas effectively, solves problems)	
4. **Displays traits/attitudes of a scientist** (is curious, questioning, persistent, precise, creative, enthusiastic; uses science materials carefully; is concerned for environment)	

Summary Evaluation/Teacher Comments: _____

_____

_____

_____

_____

Name _____
Date _____

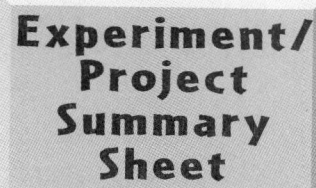

You can tell about your science project by completing the following sentences.

My Unit Experiment/Project

1. My experiment/project was about _____
   _____
   _____.

2. I worked on this experiment/project with _____
   _____
   _____.

3. I gathered information from these sources: _____
   _____
   _____.

4. The most important thing I learned from doing this experiment/project is ____
   _____
   _____.

5. I think I did a (an) _____ job on my experiment/project because
   _____
   _____.

6. I'd also like to tell you _____
   _____
   _____
   _____
   _____.

Grade 1 **Assessment Guide   AG xix**

Portfolio Assessment

A portfolio is a showcase for student work, a place where many types of assignments, projects, reports, and writings can be collected. The work samples in the collection provide "snapshots" of the student's efforts over time, and taken together they reveal the student's growth, attitudes, and understanding better than any other type of assessment. However, portfolios are not ends in themselves. Their value comes from creating them, discussing them, and using them to improve learning.

The purpose of using portfolios in science is threefold:

▶ *To give the student a voice in the assessment process.*

▶ *To foster reflection, self-monitoring, and self-evaluation.*

▶ *To provide a comprehensive picture of a student's progress.*

Portfolio Assessment in *Harcourt Science*

In *Harcourt Science*, students create portfolio collections of their work. The collection may include a few required papers, such as the Chapter Test, Chapter Performance Task, and Experiment/Project Evaluation.

From time to time, consider including other measures (Science Experiences Record, Experiment/Project Summary Sheet, and Student Self-Assessment Checklists). The Science Experiences Record, for example, can reveal insights about student interests, ideas, and out-of-school experiences (museum visits, nature walks, outside readings, and so on) that otherwise you might not know about. Materials to help you and your students build portfolios and use them for evaluation are included in the pages that follow.

Using Portfolio Assessment

▶ *Explain the portfolio and its use.*
Describe how people in many fields use portfolios to present samples of their work when they are applying for a job. Tell students that they can create their own portfolio to show what they have learned, what skills they have acquired, and how they think they are doing in science.

▶ *Decide what standard pieces should be included.*
Engage students in identifying a few standard, or "required," work samples that each student should include in his or her portfolio, and discuss reasons for including them. The student's recording sheet for the Chapter Performance Task, for example, might be a standard sample in the portfolios because it shows students' ability to use science process skills and critical thinking skills to solve a problem. Together with your class, decide on the required work samples that everyone's portfolio will include.

▶ *Discuss student-selected work samples.*
Point out that the best work to select is not necessarily the longest or the neatest. Rather, it is work the student believes will best demonstrate his or her growth in science understanding and skills.

▶ *Establish a basic plan.*
Decide about how many work samples will be included in the portfolio and when they should be selected. Ask students to list on Guide to My Science Portfolio (p. AGxxiii) each sample they select and to explain why they selected it.

▶ *Tell students how you will evaluate their portfolios.*
Use a blank Portfolio Evaluation sheet to explain how you will evaluate the contents of a portfolio.

▶ *Use the portfolio.*
Use the portfolio as a handy reference tool in determining students' science grades and in holding conferences with them and family members. You may wish to send the portfolio home for family members to review.

Name _____ Date _____

Science Experiences Record

Date	What I Did	What I Thought or Learned

GUIDE TO MY Science Portfolio

Name _____ Date _____

What Is in My Portfolio	Why I Chose It
1.	
2.	
3.	
4.	
5.	
6.	
7.	

I organized my Science Portfolio this way because _____
_____
_____
_____
_____

Grade 1

Student's Name _____
Date _____

Portfolio Evaluation Checklist

Portfolio Evaluation

Aspects of Science Literacy	Evidence of Growth
1. **Understands science concepts** (Animals, Plants; Earth's Land, Air, Water, Space; Weather; Matter, Motion, Energy)	_____
2. **Uses science process skills** (observes, compares, classifies, gathers/interprets data, communicates, measures, experiments, infers, predicts, draws conclusions)	_____
3. **Thinks critically** (analyzes, synthesizes, evaluates, applies ideas effectively, solves problems)	_____
4. **Displays traits/attitudes of a scientist** (is curious, questioning, persistent, precise, creative, enthusiastic; uses science materials carefully; is concerned for environment)	_____

Summary of Portfolio Assessment

For This Review			Since Last Review		
Excellent	Good	Fair	Improving	About the Same	Not as Good

AG xxiv Assessment GuideGrade 1

Name _____
Date _____

Living and Nonliving Things

Part 1 Vocabulary

Circle the word that answers the question.

1. What do we call hearing, sight, touch, smell, and taste?

    ears   hands   senses

Circle the word that names the pictures.

2.

    living   nonliving

3.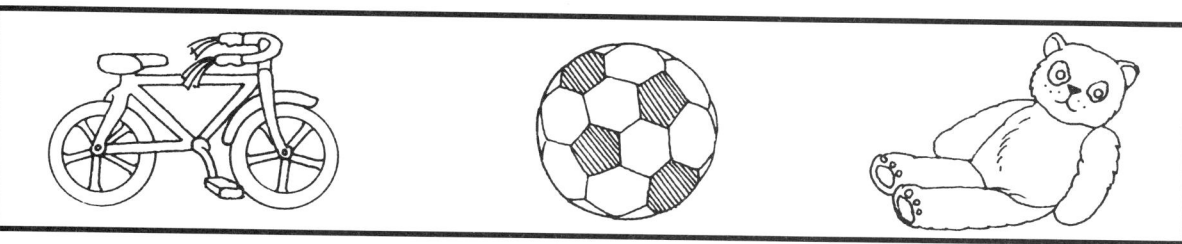

    living   nonliving

Name _____

Part II Science Concepts and Understanding

Draw a line from each sense to the child using it.

4. sight •

5. hearing •

6. touch •

7. taste •

8. smell •

Unit A • Chapter 1

Name _____

9. Circle each word that tells what these living things need.

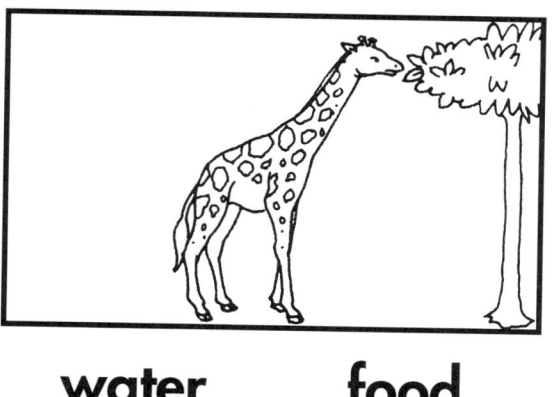 

water   food   air   water

10. Circle each word that tells what these living things do.

grows   sees   changes   hears

11. Circle the nonliving thing.

Name _____

Part III Process Skills Application

Process skills: *observe, compare*

12. Write **g** under the thing that grows.

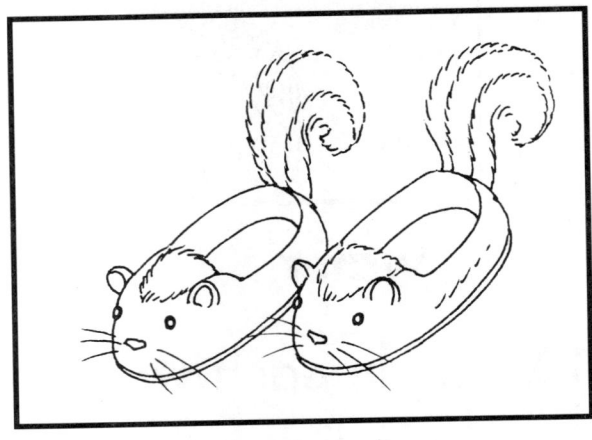

13. Write **c** under the thing that changes.

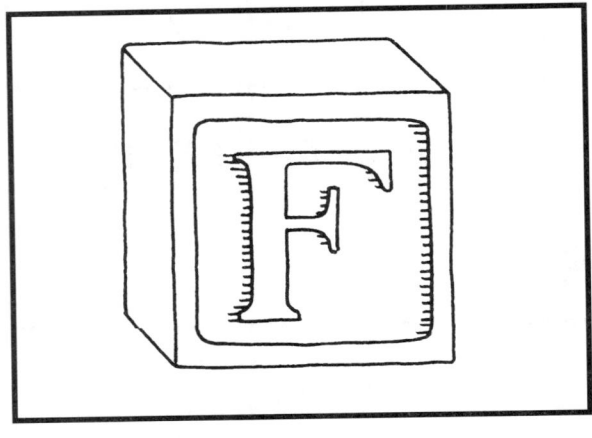

Name _____ Date _____

Living Things

Materials

picture cards

red yarn

blue yarn

crayons or markers

drawing paper

1. Make a red circle and a blue circle with the yarn.
2. Look at the pictures.
3. Put the living things in the red circle.
4. Put the nonliving things in the blue circle.
5. Draw other living and nonliving things.

Living Things   Nonliving Things

Unit A • Chapter 1   Assessment Guide   AG 5

PERFORMANCE TASK

Teacher's Directions

Living Things

Materials Performance Task sheets, picture cards, crayons or markers, drawing paper, red yarn, blue yarn

Time 20–30 minutes

Suggested Grouping individuals or pairs

Science Processes observe, compare

Preparation Hints Cut the lengths of yarn ahead of time. Have a parent or volunteer cut out pictures for children to use.

Introduce the Task Have children look around the classroom and name the living and nonliving things that they see. Encourage them to say what the living things can do. Distribute materials. Read the five directions to children. Be sure that they understand how to make their circles and what they should put in them.

Promote Discussion Have children compare their pictures of living and nonliving things. Then encourage children to say what the living things do.

Scoring Rubric

Performance Indicators

_____ Places pictures of things that are living within the red circle.

_____ Places pictures of things that are nonliving within the blue circle.

_____ Draws pictures of living and nonliving things.

_____ Compares pictures with classmates and tells what the living things can do.

Observations and Rubric Score

| 3 | 2 | 1 | 0 |

Name _____
Date _____

All About Plants

Part 1 Vocabulary

Circle the word or words that complete each sentence.

1. Most plants grow from a

    flower   stem   seed

2. The outside of a seed is its

    stem   seed coat   flower

Draw a line from the name of each plant part to its picture.

3. leaves •

4. flower •

5. roots •

6. stem •

7. Put an **X** on the sunlight.

Unit A • Chapter 2   (page 1 of 4)   Assessment Guide   AG 7

Name _____

Part II   Science Concepts and Understanding

We eat parts of some plants.

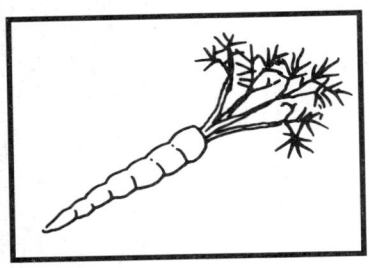  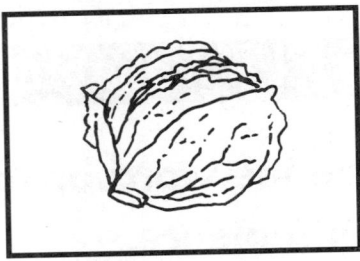

carrot　　　　　**apple**　　　　　**lettuce**

Write a word or draw a picture to answer the question.

8. Which plant above has a root we eat?

_____
_ _ _ _ _ _ _ _ _ _ _ _ _ _ _
_____

9. Circle the word that tells what this plant needs.

light　　　　**water**　　　　**air**

Name _____

10. Circle what the flowers under the tree need.

air   water   light

11. Number the pictures to show how a plant grows.

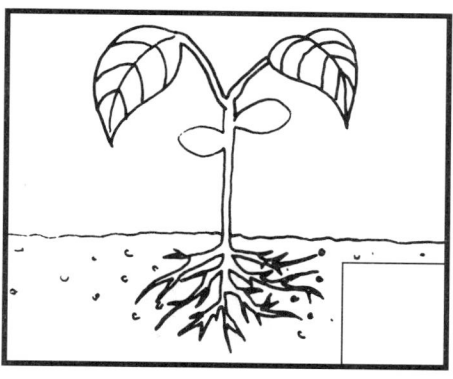 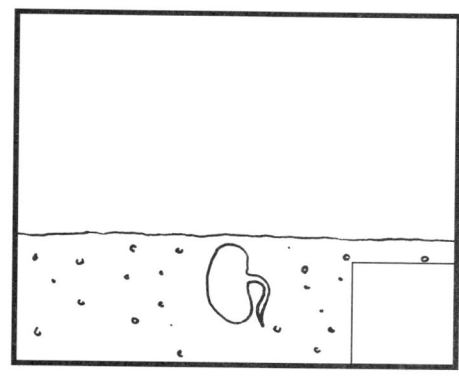

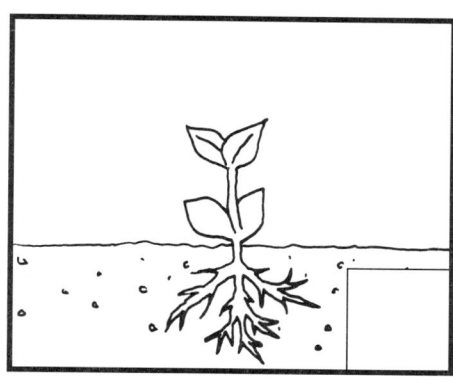 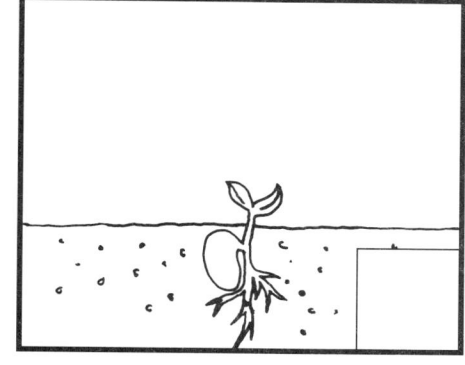

Name _____

Part III Process Skills Application

Process skills: observe, compare

12. Put an **X** under the plant whose seed was planted first.

  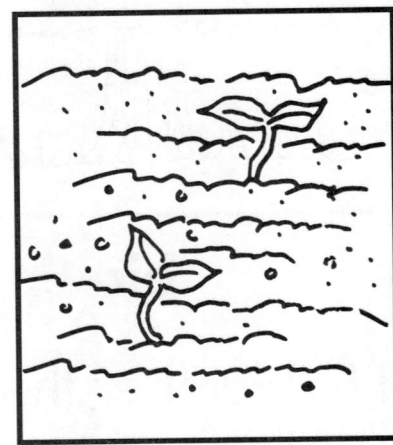

_____   _____   _____

13. Circle the word that tells what is falling from this tree.

stems

leaves

roots

Name _____   Date _____

How Plants Grow

Materials

 scissors    glue    crayons   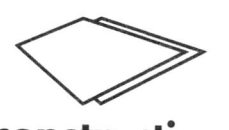 construction paper

1. Draw a picture that shows all the parts of a plant.

2. Then cut and paste the words to name the parts of your picture.

3. Tell your teacher which part of your plant grows first, next, and last.

air	sunlight	water	roots
stem	leaves	flowers	

Unit A • Chapter 2   Assessment Guide   AG 11

Teacher's Directions

How Plants Grow

Materials — Performance Task sheets, construction paper, crayons, scissors, glue

Time — 20–30 minutes

Suggested Grouping — individuals, pairs, or small groups

Science Processes — observe, compare, communicate

Preparation Hints — If possible, take children outside or display a live plant for children to observe. Have children share what they know about the parts of the plant and how it grows.

Introduce the Task — Explain to children that their task is to draw any plant they choose and to use the words on the Performance Task sheet to label all the parts of their picture. When they are finished with their drawing, they will use it to explain which part of the plant grows first, next, and so on.

Promote Discussion — When children finish, have them compare their work. Ask the class to summarize how different kinds of plants grow.

Scoring Rubric

Performance Indicators

____ Makes an accurate drawing of a plant, showing roots, leaves, stems, and flowers.

____ Labels each part of the drawing by pasting the appropriate word next to each part.

____ Uses proper sequence to clearly explain how a plant grows.

____ Compares his or her own drawing with those of classmates.

Observations and Rubric Score

| 3 | 2 | 1 | 0 |

Name _____
Date _____

All About Animals

Part 1   Vocabulary

Draw a line from each word to the picture that matches it.

1. mammal
2. amphibian
3. reptile
4. gills
5. tadpole
6. insect
7. pupa
8. hatch
9. larva

Name _____

Part II Science Concepts and Understanding

10. Circle what all animals need.

   wings   food   fins

11. Circle what helps some animals get air.

   feet   fur   noses

12. Circle the animal that builds a nest.

13. Put an **X** on the part of the animal that helps it get water.

AG 14 Assessment Guide Unit A • Chapter 3

Name _____

14. Circle the word that tells what is in the picture.

reptiles

mammals

15. Circle something that only birds have.

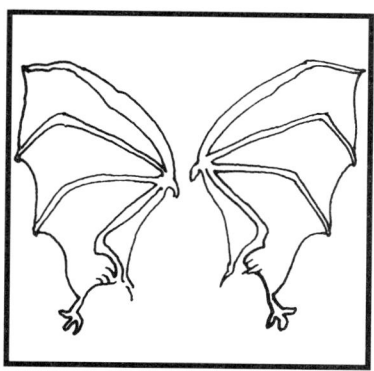 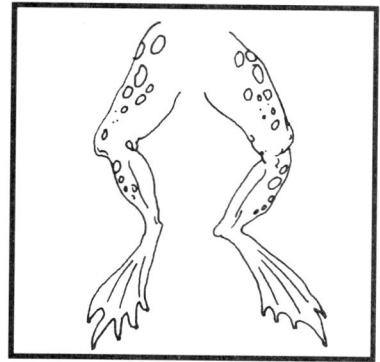 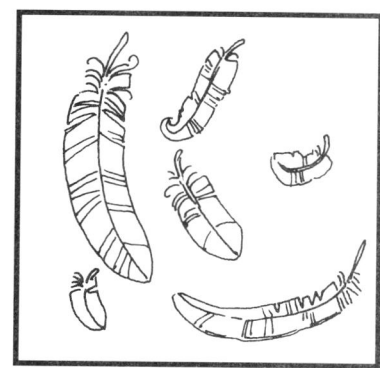

16. Circle something that only mammals have.

feet   fur   wings

Name _____

Part III   Process Skills Application

Process Skills: sequence, classify

17. Number the pictures to show how a butterfly grows.

 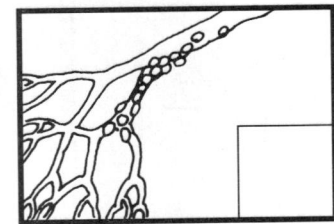

 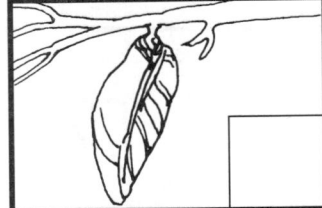

Circle the word to classify each animal.

18.	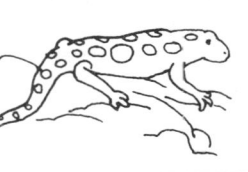	has six legs	**mammal** **insect**
19.		has wet skin	**bird** **amphibian**
20.		has gills	**reptile** **fish**

AG 16   Assessment Guide   (page 4 of 4)   Unit A • Chapter 3

Name _____ Date _____

Animal Watch

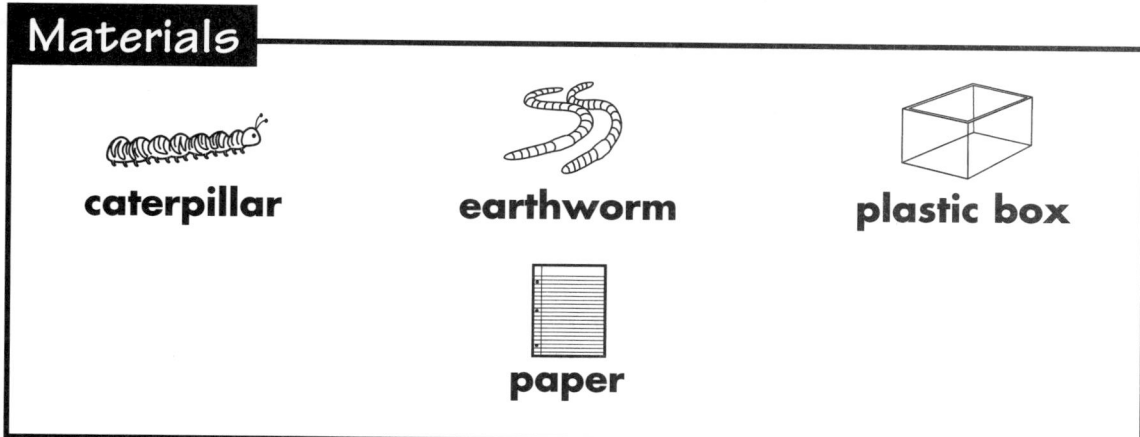

1. Observe the animals in the plastic box.

2. Write their names on your paper.

3. Compare the two animals. Write two ways they are the same and different.

4. Share what you wrote on your paper.

Animals	Same	Different
Caterpillar and Earthworm	1. 2.	1. 2.

PERFORMANCE TASK

Teacher's Directions

Animal Watch

Materials — Performance Task sheets, caterpillar, earthworm, plastic box, paper, pencils, several animal picture cards

Time — 20–30 minutes

Suggested Grouping — individuals, pairs, or small groups

Science Processes — observe, compare, communicate

Preparation Hints — Put the earthworm and the caterpillar in the box. Put the picture cards on the chalk ledge. Have the remaining materials ready.

Introduce the Task — Display the animal picture cards one at a time. Encourage children to brainstorm ways to describe each animal. Distribute materials. Read the first direction aloud. Make sure children can identify the animals. Tell children that they will have a chance to describe what is the same and different about the animals. Read directions 2–4 to children. Have volunteers explain what they will do and how they will share the information on their papers.

Promote Discussion — Ask individuals what was the same and different about the animals. Have them count differences class members described.

Scoring Rubric

Performance Indicators

_____ Lists two ways in which the animals are the same.

_____ Lists two ways in which the animals are different.

_____ Writes a clear description of the animals' similarities and differences.

_____ Explains clearly the similarities and differences.

Observations and Rubric Score

| 3 | 2 | 1 | 0 |

Name _____
Date _____

Plants and Animals All Around
Circle the correct answer.

1. Which body part do you use for hearing?

   eye   mouth   ear

2. What sense tells you how something looks?

   smell   taste   sight

3. Which is nonliving?

4. Where do plant seeds come from?

Name _____

5. A plant's roots take in _____.

    soil   **water**   **sunlight**

6. What part makes food for a plant?

 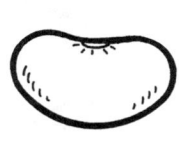 

7. What do you plant to grow new plants?

    eggs   **flowers**   **seeds**

8. What do plants need to live?

    water   **wind**   **rocks**

9. Plants need air and _____ to make food.

    soil   **sunlight**   **people**

10. Animals need food, water, air, and a place to _____.

    live   **eat**   **run**

Name _____

11. What do fish use to breathe?

nose　　　　**lungs**　　　　gills

12. Which is a mammal?

13. Which is an amphibian?

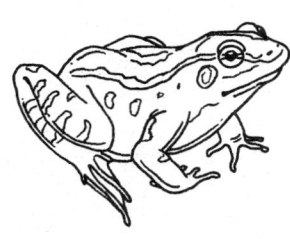 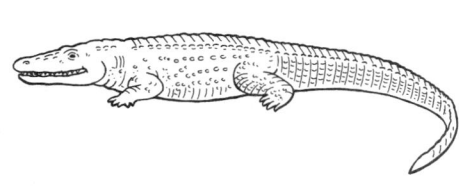 

14. Which is an insect?

ant　　　　**frog**　　　　**salamander**

15. Snakes are a type of _____.

bird　　　　**mammal**　　　　reptile

Name _____

16. Chicks _____ out of eggs.

    eat   taste   hatch

17. Which picture shows an animal caring for its young?

18. Which grows inside a pupa?

19. What is another word for a caterpillar?

    larva   butterfly   tadpole

20. A young frog is a _____.

    chick   tadpole   larva

Name _____
Date _____

Plants and Animals Need One Another

Part 1 Vocabulary

Circle the word that answers the question.

1. What is the powder on flowers that helps make seeds?

    dust   pollen   hair

2. What is the basket?

    clothing   a product

3. What do leaves and worms do for the soil?

    dry it   water it   enrich it

4. What do these animals use the tree for?

    water   shelter

Unit B • Chapter 1   (page 1 of 4)   Assessment Guide AG 23

Name _____

Part II Science Concepts and Understanding

These animals are meeting their needs with grass. Circle the word that tells what need they are meeting.

5.

water

shelter

6.

air

food

These animals are helping plants. Circle the words that tell what they are doing.

7.

moving pollen

finding water

8.

making a nest

spreading seeds

Name _____

Draw a line from each picture to what the plants or animals give people.

9.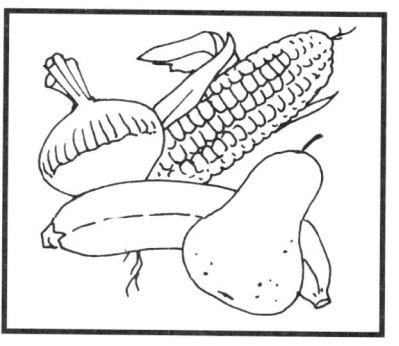

10.

• food

• shelter

11.

• beauty

12.

Unit B • Chapter 1

Name _____

Part III   Process Skills Application

Process skills: observe, investigate, classify

Circle the word that tells what each product comes from.

13.

animals

plants

14.

animals

plants

15. Circle the words that tell what the dog is doing for the woman.

hearing for her

seeing for her

16. Write the word that tells what each product comes from.

plant

animal

_____   _____

Name _____ Date _____

How Animals Use Plants

Materials

- markers or crayons
- index cards
- lined paper

This picture shows a squirrel using a plant to meet its needs. Which of its needs is the animal meeting?

1. List three plants that three animals use to meet their needs.

2. Make a picture card to show each animal using its plant.

3. Show each card and tell how the animal is using the plant.

Unit B • Chapter 1

Assessment Guide AG 27

PERFORMANCE TASK

Teacher's Directions

How Animals Use Plants

Materials — Performance Task sheets, markers or crayons, index cards, lined paper

Time — 20–30 minutes

Suggested Grouping — individuals or small groups

Science Processes — communicate, observe

Preparation Hints — Count out the cards for each child ahead of time. You may wish to cut construction paper into 4-in. × 6-in. pieces.

Introduce the Task — Ask children how a bird uses a tree. Elicit that the tree can be a home; the bird uses it to meet its need for shelter. Ask children to suggest other plants that animals use for food and for water. Distribute the materials. Read aloud the title and the paragraph under it. Have a volunteer answer the question. (It is meeting its need for shelter.) Read the directions with children. Have volunteers tell what they will put on their lists and draw on the cards. Tell children to write their lists on the lined paper. Remind them to share the cards when they finish.

Promote Discussion — When children finish, have them show the class another child's card and explain how the animal pictured is using the plant.

Scoring Rubric

Performance Indicators

_____ Lists several plants that animals use.

_____ Draws pictures that accurately depict how the animals use the plants listed.

_____ Explains clearly how the animals use the plants to meet their needs.

_____ Explains what is happening on another child's picture card.

Observations and Rubric Score

| 3 | 2 | 1 | 0 |

Name _____
Date _____

A Place to Live

Part 1   Vocabulary

Draw a line to the word or words that complete each sentence.

1. A dry place that gets a lot of sunlight and very little rain is a •

2. A place where the soil is moist and many trees grow is a •

3. A place that is wet all year and has many trees is a •

4. A large body of salt water is an •

5. Seaweed is a kind of •

- • **forest**
- • **desert**
- • **rain forest**
- • **ocean**
- • **algae**

Unit B • Chapter 2   (page 1 of 4)   Assessment Guide   AG 29

Name _____

Part II Science Concepts and Understanding

Circle the answer to each question.

6. What helps these plants grow in the forest?

moist soil

dry soil

7. What do these animals find in the forest?

shelter

seaweed

8. What can these desert plants hold in their leaves and stems?

soil

water

AG 30 Assessment Guide (page 2 of 4) Unit B • Chapter 2

Name _____

Circle the words or picture to answer each question.

9. Where do some desert animals get water?

   from oceans   from plants

10. Which animal lives in the middle level of the rain forest?

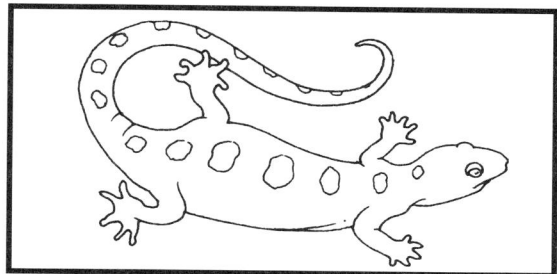   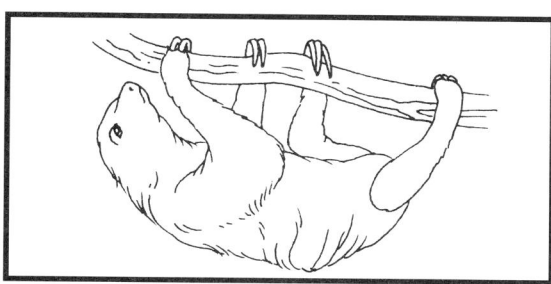

11. What covers more than half of Earth?

    land   oceans

12. What do plants in the middle level of the rain forest get?

    cold   light

Name _____

Part III   Process Skills Application

Process Skills: classify, compare

13. Write letters to complete this chart. The top row has been done for you.

d = desert   o = ocean
f = forest   r = rain forest

Animal	Plant or Plantlike	Where They Live
(parrot)	(orchid)	r
(raccoon)	(tree)	
(armadillo)	(cactus)	
(starfish)	(seaweed)	

14. Circle the part of the sea turtle that helps it steer.

shell

flippers

Name _____ Date _____

Who Lives Here?

Materials

- toothpicks
- chenille sticks
- construction paper
- seeds
- markers
- foam ball
- bottle caps
- string
- straws

Places to Live

forest   desert

rain forest   ocean

1. Choose one of the places to live.

2. List body parts an animal needs to live there.

3. Make a model of an animal that could live there.

4. Share your model.

PERFORMANCE TASK

Teacher's Directions

Who Lives Here?

Materials Performance Task sheets, toothpicks, chenille sticks, scraps of construction paper, foam ball, seeds, markers, bottle caps, string, straws

Time 20–30 minutes

Suggested Grouping pairs or small groups

Science Processes classify, communicate

Preparation Hints Sort a variety of materials into small bags—one for each child. Place additional materials on a table for children to use.

Introduce the Task Have children think about forest animals and the body parts that help them meet their needs in the forest. Ask children to name animals that live in other places and tell how their body parts help them meet their needs there. Be sure they mention animals of the desert, rain forest, and ocean. Distribute materials. Read aloud the title of the Performance Task and the list of Places to Live. Then help children read the directions.

Promote Discussion Have children who selected the same place to live compare their animals. Ask the groups to report on how their animals' body parts help them meet their needs.

Scoring Rubric
Performance Indicators

___ Lists more than one adaptation an animal needs in order to live in the place selected.

___ Explains clearly what adaptations an animal needs and why.

___ Makes a model of an animal from scrap material.

___ Explains to the class how each part of the animal helps it to live in the place selected. For example, their model may show an animal that has strong toenails needed to climb trees.

Observations and Rubric Score

| 3 | 2 | 1 | 0 |

Name _____
Date _____

Living Together

Circle the correct answer.

1. Which picture shows an animal using shelter?

2. Which animal eats both plants and animals?

   cow   rabbit   raccoon

3. Which animal is doing something that helps plants?

Unit B   (page 1 of 4)   Assessment Guide AG 35

Name _____

4. Which product is made from an animal?

    cotton balls   wool sweater   peanut butter

5. Where would you find many trees?

    desert   forest   ocean

6. Which would forest animals eat?

7. Which animal could live in the desert?

Name _____

8. Which word tells about a desert?

wet   **dry**   **shady**

9. Where do orchids grow in a rain forest?

forest floor   **halfway up the trees**   **top of the canopy**

10. What word goes with this picture?

desert   **ocean**   **rain forest**

Name _____

Circle the word or words that belong in the blank.

11. Worms can _____ the soil.

    destroy   **enrich**   **water**

12. A butterfly can help plants by carrying _____.

    seeds   **flowers**   **pollen**

13. Paper is a _____ made from plants.

    stage   **leaf**   **product**

14. A _____ is a warm, wet place with many trees.

    rain forest   **ocean**   **desert**

15. Seaweed is a type of _____.

    tree   **animal**   **algae**

Name _____
Date _____

Earth's Land

Part 1 Vocabulary

Circle the word that answers each question.

1. What is a hard, nonliving thing?

    rock   **tree**

2. What is made of very tiny pieces of rock?

    soil   **sand**

3. What are bones and imprints of animals that lived long ago?

    seashells   **fossils**

4. What word tells that a kind of plant or animal is gone forever?

    asleep   **extinct**

Name _____

Part II Science Concepts and Understanding

Circle the letter next to the word that completes each sentence.

5. One way to sort rocks is by their

   A smell   **B** color   **C** sound

6. Glass products are made from

   F sand   **G** water   **H** air

7. An imprint of an extinct plant is a

   A starfish   **B** rock   **C** fossil

8. What can people make from rocks?

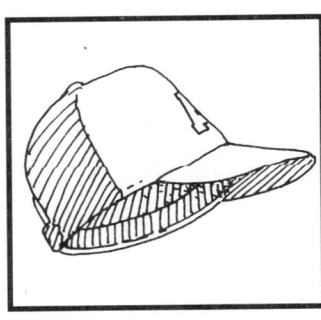  

   F   **G**   **H**

Name _____

9. Draw something that people use sand to make.

[ ]

10. Complete the chart. Write L for living and N for nonliving.

rock	N
child	___
sand	___
fossil	___

11. What could help a dead plant or dead animal become a fossil? _____
_____
_____

Name _____

Part III   Process Skills Application

Process skills: compare, classify

12. Circle the words that tell about each of these things.

What Are They Like?			
rocks	smooth	rough	soft
fossils	hot	old	hard
sand	bits of rock	bits of plant	bits of glass

Draw a line to match each kind of fossil to something we learn from it.

13. fossil bones •   • kind of food the animal ate

14. fossil teeth •   • how big the animal was

15. fossil cone •   • where water covered the land

16. fossil shell •   • kind of seeds the plant had

Name _____ Date _____

Water Test

PERFORMANCE TASK

Materials

- 6 paper cups
- water
- potting soil
- small rocks
- sand
- marker

1. Make a hole in the bottom of three cups.

2. Put rocks in one cup, sand in another, and potting soil in the last cup.

3. Write **R** on an empty cup. Hold the cup of rocks over it. Pour water through the rocks.

4. Write **S** and **P** on two more empty cups. Pour water through the sand and potting soil over these cups.

5. Compare the amounts of water in the cups. Put the cups in order from most to least.

PERFORMANCE TASK

Teacher's Directions

Water Test

Materials — Performance Task sheets, paper cups, marker, rocks, sand, potting soil, water

Time — 20–30 minutes

Suggested Grouping — pairs or small groups

Science Processes — compare, order, infer

Preparation Hints — You may wish to have a volunteer measure out the sand, rocks, and potting soil for each group ahead of time.

Introduce the Task — Distribute a cup of rocks, sand, and potting soil to each group. On the chalkboard, write *How Are They Alike? How Are They Different?* Help children compare the three materials. Record their suggestions on the chalkboard. Explain to the class that they will do an investigation to find another way the materials are different. Help children read the directions for the Water Test, restating in their own words what they are to do. Then distribute a container of water to each group.

Promote Discussion — When children finish, ask them to report on what they observed. Then call on volunteers to represent rocks, sand, and potting soil. Have them arrange themselves in the order of the amounts of water that drain through the three types of soil. Ask students to infer why potted plants grow better in potting soil than in rocks and sand.

Scoring Rubric

Performance Indicators

_____ Compares the amounts of water that drained through the three types of soil.

_____ Orders the cups from greatest to least amount of water and explains their order.

_____ Infers that plants grow better in potting soil because it holds water longer around their roots.

Observations and Rubric Score

| 3 | 2 | 1 | 0 |

AG 44 *Assessment Guide* — Unit C • Chapter 1

Name _____
Date _____

Our Natural Resources

Part 1   Vocabulary

Draw a line from the word to the place on the map that it names.

1. lake •

2. river •

3. stream •

Circle the word that best completes the sentence.

4. The water in rivers is
   salt water   fresh water

5. Something in nature that people use is a
   natural resource   machine

6. Most cans and pans are made from
   minerals   garnets

Name _____

7. What we feel when the wind blows is

        air   clouds

Draw a line to show what each word means.

How We Help Save Natural Resources
8. reuse •   • use less of something
9. recycle •   • use something again
10. reduce •   • collect things so they can be made into new things

Part II Science Concepts and Understanding

11. What do people recycle?

   A milk and soft drinks
   B cans and newspapers
   C sidewalks and streets

Name _____

12. Circle the picture that does **NOT** show air moving.

Draw a line to show how you could reuse each thing.

13. milk jug • • make a pencil holder

14. aluminum can • • make a sand scoop

15. What kind of water falls as rain?

 _____

Circle the word that best completes the sentence.

16. Before people drink water, they must make sure it is

      cold   clean

Name _____

Part III Process Skills Application

Process skills: infer, communicate

17. Circle the word that tells what is in the bubbles.

    water   air

Circle the letter of the best answer.

18. Which is **NOT** made from trees?

    A tables   **B** newspapers   **C** minerals

19. Which thing has no air in it?

    F water   **G** rock   **H** soil

20. Which sense helps you know the air is moving?

    A sight   **B** taste   **C** smell

Name _____ Date _____

Animal Kites

Materials

 construction paper   string   paper

 markers or crayons  scissors   tape

 tissue-paper streamers

Day	Wind?	What the Kite Did

1. Draw an animal big enough to be a kite. Cut it out.

2. Tape streamers and a string to your animal.

3. Take your kite outside. Hold it by the string.

4. Fly your kite every day for a week. Write down what happens.

5. Make a chart to share what you learn.

PERFORMANCE TASK

Teacher's Directions

Animal Kites

Materials construction paper, 12-in. pieces of string, markers or crayons, tissue-paper streamers, scissors, tape, Performance Assessment sheets, pencils, paper

Time 20–30 minutes

Suggested Grouping individuals or small groups

Science Processes observe, infer, communicate

Preparation Hints Make enough streamers for each child to have several.

Introduce the Task Ask children what clues they can look for out the classroom window to find out whether the wind is blowing and how hard it is blowing (for example, papers or leaves blowing across the schoolyard, leaves on trees blowing, people holding onto their hats). Explain that they will be making animal kites that will show whether the wind is blowing and how hard it is blowing. Distribute the Performance Assessment sheets. Help children read the materials list, and have them look at the picture. Ask if they can tell how they will use the materials to make their kites. Help them read the directions. Let children make their kites, take them out to try them, and remind them to record the results. Repeat the procedure each day for a week.

Promote Discussion At the end of the week, ask children to report what happened each day.

Scoring Rubric

Performance Indicators

_____ Assembles the kite successfully.
_____ Carries out the experiment daily.
_____ Records results accurately.
_____ Makes an accurate chart and uses it to report to the class about flying the kite.

Observations and Rubric Score

| 3 | 2 | 1 | 0 |

Name _____

Date _____

About Our Earth

Circle the letter of the correct answer.

1. What do you call tiny broken pieces of rock?

    A shells   **B** sand   **C** statues

2. Which word tells about rocks?

    F living   **G** extinct   **H** nonliving

3. What can be made from sand?

    A rock   **B** glass   **C** paper

4. Which word goes with this picture?

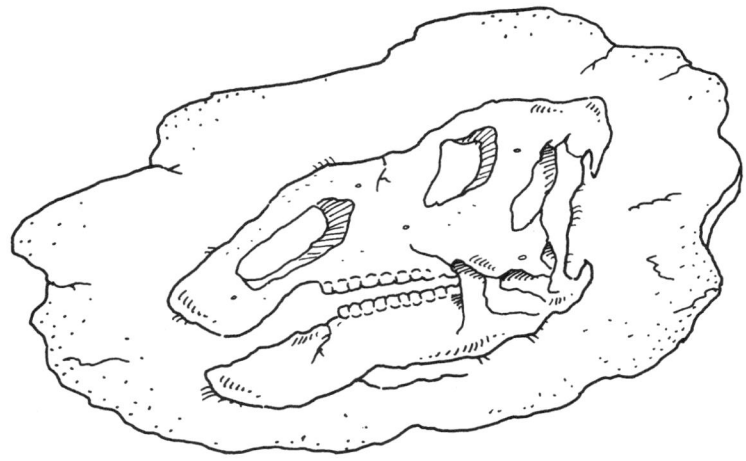

   F mineral   **G** sand   **H** fossil

Name _____

5. Which word tells about a kind of plant that is no longer living?

   A natural   **B** extinct   **C** mineral

6. Which picture shows a natural resource?

   F   **G**   **H**

7. A cooking pot is made from which natural resource?

   A tree   **B** water   **C** mineral

Name _____

8. Which picture shows a lake?

F  **G**  **H**

9. Where would you find salt water?

A lakes **B** forests **C** oceans

10. When you collect used things so they can be made into new things you _____.

F reduce **G** recycle **H** waste

Name _____

Write the answer in the blank.

| fresh water   air   fossils |
| reduce   natural resources |

11. You can learn how plants and animals have changed by comparing them with _____.

12. Minerals, water, and forests are kinds of _____.

13. A natural resource that you can't see, smell, or taste is _____.

14. Water that is not salty is _____.

15. When you use a lunch box, you _____ your use of paper.

Name _____
Date _____

Measuring Weather

Part I   Vocabulary

Draw a line from each picture to a word or words for it.

1. 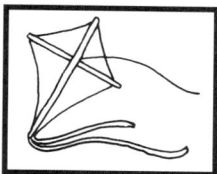 •   • water cycle

2.  •   • weather

3.  •   • thermometer

4.  •   • wind

Write the word or words that best complete the sentence.

| water vapor   evaporate   temperature   condense |

5. We call how warm or cold something is its
_____
- -
_____ .

Unit D • Chapter 1   (page 1 of 4)   Assessment Guide   AG 55

Name _____

6. Water that you can not see in the air is _____.

7. Warm air makes water _____.

8. Cooler air makes water vapor _____.

Part II   Science Concepts and Understanding

9. What does a meteorologist study? _____

Circle the letter of the word that best completes the sentence.

10. At night, with no sunlight, the air feels

    A cloudy   **B** cooler   **C** warmer

Name _____

11. Circle the letter of the city **MOST** likely to get rain.

F   G   H

Write the word or words that best complete each sentence.

| rain | water vapor | condenses | evaporates |

12. On a hot day, water _____.

13. When the drops of water in a cloud get heavy, they fall as _____.

14. Water in the air that you can not see is _____.

15. When water vapor meets cooler air, it _____.

Name _____

Part III Process Skills Application

Process skills: *observe, compare*

16. Circle the picture that shows a windy day.

17. Circle the words that tell where the weather is warmer.

Hal's city   Ann's city

Name _____ Date _____

Weather Watcher

Materials

construction paper

crayons or markers

1. Make a book to record the weather for one week.

2. Fold three sheets of paper in half. You will have a cover and five pages.

3. Observe the weather each day. Tell about it in your book.

4. Record the outside temperature.

5. Draw a picture to show what the weather is like.

6. Share your book with the class.

PERFORMANCE TASK

Teacher's Directions

Weather Watcher

Materials   Performance Task sheets, construction paper, crayons or markers, thermometer, stapler or hole punch and yarn

Time   10–15 minutes each day

Suggested Grouping   individuals or small groups

Science Processes   observe, communicate, use numbers, use time/space relationships

Preparation Hints   Show children how to fold three sheets of construction paper in half to make a 6-page book. Staple their pages on the fold, or punch holes so they can tie them with yarn. Have them write *Weather Watcher* on the cover and label each page with the name of a school day. Place a thermometer outside the window for them to read daily.

Introduce the Task   Review with the class some different types of weather and what temperature means. Explain to children that they will be keeping a weather-watcher log. Read the directions to the children. Guide children through the first page by discussing the weather outside. Encourage them to observe the clouds, the movement of trees by the wind, the way people are dressed, etc. Repeat daily until the book is completed.

Promote Discussion   Ask children to share their books. Have them summarize the kinds of weather they observed in the past week.

Scoring Rubric

Performance Indicators

____ Records daily outside temperature.

____ Describes weather daily with appropriate words such as *windy*, *cloudy*, or *rainy*.

____ Draws appropriate pictures to show what the weather is like outside.

____ Shares observations with class by summarizing observed weather.

Observations and Rubric Score

| 3 | 2 | 1 | 0 |

Name _____
Date _____

The Sky and the Seasons

Part 1 Vocabulary

Write the letter of the word that belongs with each picture.

| **A** fall | **B** winter | **C** spring | **D** summer |

1. ___   2. ___   3. ___   4. ___

Write the letter of the best choice.

___ 5. Brightest object in the night sky

___ 6. Far away objects that give off light

___ 7. Makes the sky bright in the daytime

___ 8. Spins like a top

___ 9. A time of year

A stars
B sun
C moon
D season
E rotates

Unit D • Chapter 2

Name _____

Part II   Science Concepts and Understanding

Circle the word that completes the sentence.

10. We have day and night because Earth

    rotates   stands still

11. Earth has four

    months   seasons

12. Earth travels around the

    moon   sun

13. The moon travels around

    Earth   the stars

14. The sun is our closest

    star   moon

Name _____

For Questions 15–17, draw a line from what a farmer does to the right season for it.

What a Farmer Does   The Season

15. picks apples and pumpkins   •   • summer

16. plants seeds   •   • spring

17. takes care of crops as they grow   •   • fall

18. In which season do we see plants beginning to come out of the ground?

_____
_____

Name _____

Part III Process Skills Application

Process Skills: order, predict, investigate

The graph below shows the hours of light in a day.

19. Put an **X** on the name of the season that has the most hours of daylight.

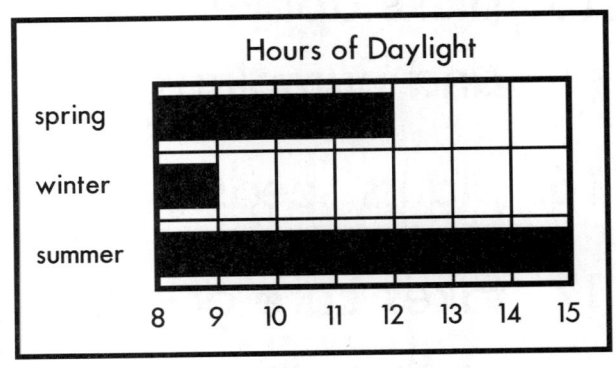

20. In which season will this squirrel look for what it is burying?

_____
_____

21. Put an **X** by the best way to investigate what will grow from a seed.

___ Plant it. Put it near a window. Water it.

___ Cut it in half. Observe.

___ Try to find the seed in a book about plants.

Name _____ Date _____

Light and Temperature

Materials

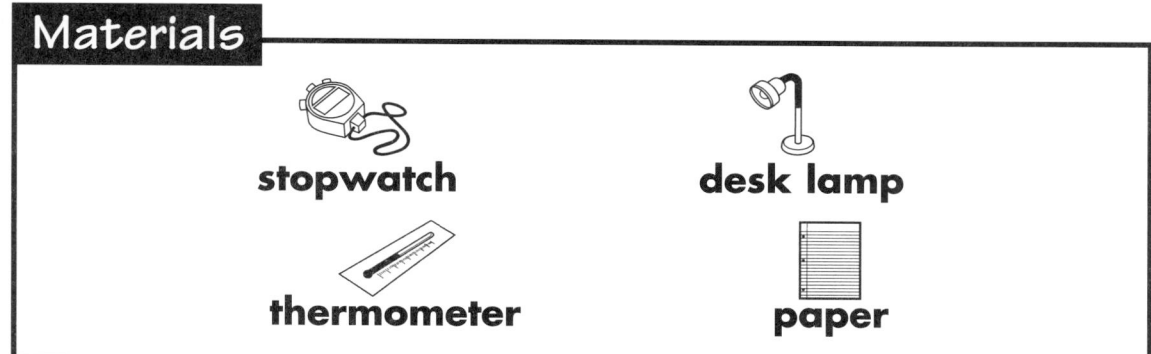

Work with a partner.

1. Make a chart like this.

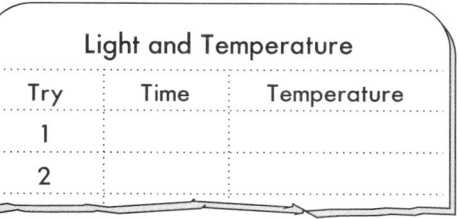

2. Place a thermometer under a lamp.

3. One person turns on the lamp. The other starts the stopwatch.

4. Try short and longer times. Record the time and temperature each time.

5. Tell what you observed.

Unit D • Chapter 2

PERFORMANCE TASK

Teacher's Directions

Light and Temperature

Materials — Performance Task sheets, stopwatch, desk lamp, thermometer, paper

Time — 20–30 minutes

Suggested Grouping — pairs

Science Processes — order, communicate

Preparation Hints — Assemble the materials. Determine the intervals of time for each try. You may wish to use 10 seconds, 30 seconds, 1 minute, and 2 minutes.

Introduce the Task — Put the headings *Summer* and *Winter* on the board. Ask volunteers to write differences they notice in the seasons (for example, in the clothing they wear, in what they can play outdoors). Be sure children think about how long the days seem during each season. Distribute materials. Read the directions aloud, and then have volunteers explain what each direction tells them to do. Repeat the activity several times, and have children record their results.

Promote Discussion — Have children share the results of their investigations. Ask them during which time period the temperature was the hottest (the longest period). Lead them to understand that the longer the period of light, the higher the temperature. Help children relate this to summer, when the days are longest and the temperatures are hottest.

Scoring Rubric
Performance Indicators

_____ Makes accurate chart for data.
_____ Turns light on and off correctly for each listed period of time.
_____ Records data on sheet accurately.
_____ Reports results to the class clearly.

Observations and Rubric Score

| 3 | 2 | 1 | 0 |

Unit D • Chapter 2

Name _____
Date _____

Unit Assessment

Weather, the Sky, and Seasons

Write the letter of the correct answer.

___ 1. What would you use to measure temperature?

A   **B**   **C**

  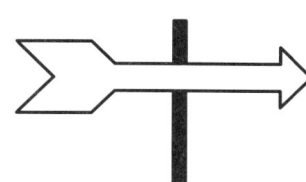

___ 2. Which thermometer shows the warmest temperature?

F   **G**   **H**

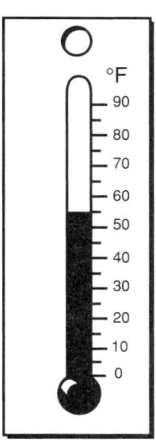 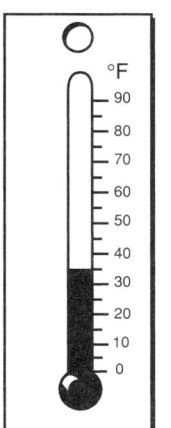 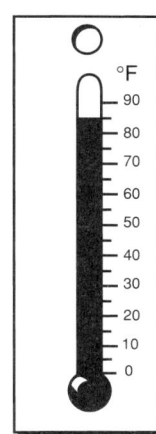

Unit D

Name _____

___ 3. Which picture shows part of the water cycle?

A 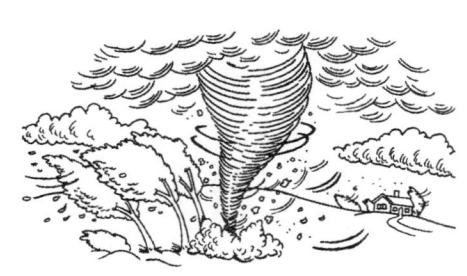 **B**  **C**

___ 4. What is something you see in the sky at night?

F sun **G** moon **H** Earth

___ 5. Where does Earth's heat and light come from?

A the sun **B** the wind **C** the moon

___ 6. Which tells why Earth has night and day?

F water cycle **G** evaporates **H** rotates

Name _____

___ 7. When do most animals give birth to young?

    A winter   **B** spring   **C** summer

___ 8. What do children do in the summer?

    F rake leaves   **G** swim outdoors   **H** go sledding

___ 9. What happens in the fall?

    A snow falls   **B** leaves fall   **C** temperatures rise

___ 10. What happens to the water in a puddle on a sunny day?

    F It gets deeper.   **G** It goes into a lake.   **H** It goes into the air.

Name _____

___ 11. Which picture shows winter?

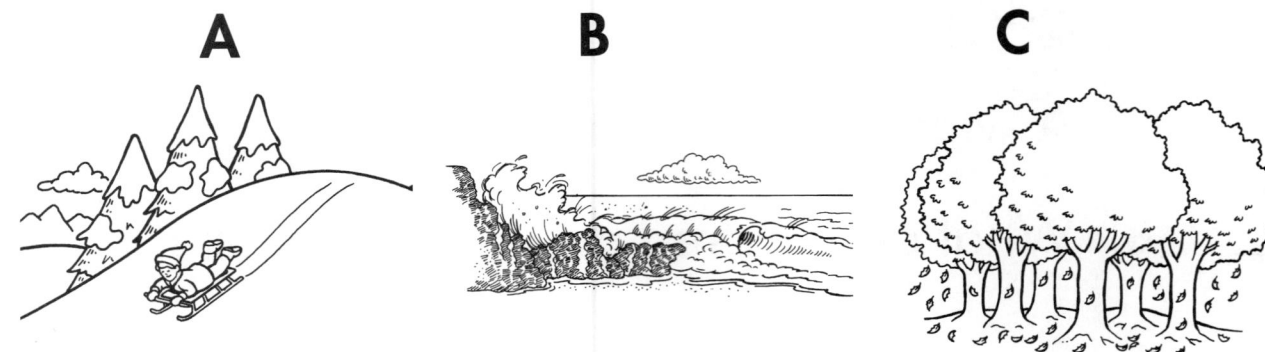

A   B   C

Write the answer in the blank.

| water vapor | weather |
| wind | seasons |

12. Spring, summer, winter, and fall are all names of _____.

13. The words cloudy, snowy, or cold all tell about the _____.

14. Water in the air that you can not see is _____.

15. Moving air that helps to fly a kite is called _____.

Name _____

Date _____

Investigate Matter

Part 1   Vocabulary

Write the letter of the word that best completes the sentence.

A change	C gas	E liquid	G sink
B floats	D matter	F dissolve	H solid

The air that fills the tube is a **1.** ___.
The tube keeps its shape, so it is a **2.** ___.
The tube **3.** ___ on the top of a **4.** ___.
The goggles **5.** ___ to the bottom.
Salt can **6.** ___ in water.
Everything in the picture is **7.** ___
You can **8.** ___ an object by bending it.

Unit E • Chapter 1   (page 1 of 4)   Assessment Guide   AG 71

Name _____

Part II Science Concepts and Understanding

Circle the letter of the best answer.

9. How are these solids sorted?

 A by shape
 B by sound
 C by color

10. What is a way to measure liquids?

 F by color
 G by shape
 H by amount

11. Which liquids do **NOT** mix?

 A vinegar and water
 B oil and water
 C milk and water

12. Which object will float?

 F an anchor
 G a cork
 H a ball of clay

13. What is inside a beach ball that helps it float?

 _____
 _____

Name _____

Draw a line to what will happen.

14. If you fill a jar with water, •

15. If you fill a jar with marbles, •

16. If you fill a jar with gas, •

• it will fill up the space in in the jar.

• it will take the shape of the jar.

• they will keep their shape.

17. Write two ways to classify these objects.

by _____   by _____

Name _____

Part III   Process Skills Application

Process skills: collect and record data, draw conclusions

18. Put an **X** below the words that tell what does **NOT** mix.

warm water   warm water   oil and
and cold water   and ice cubes   water

_____   _____   _____

19. Look at the bottles. Make a tally mark for each bottle.

A   **B**   **C**   **D**   **E**

Matter

	A	B	C	D	E	Total
Solid						
Liquid						
Gas						

Name _____ Date _____

Mix and See

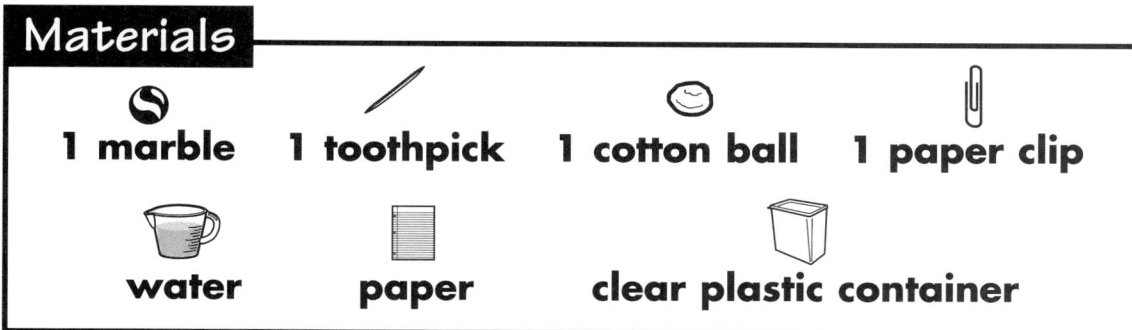

1. You will put four things into water.

2. Tell what you think will happen to each.

3. Put each thing in the water. Then write **yes** or **no** to show what happened.

The Water Test

	Keeps Shape	Loses Shape	Sinks	Floats
Cotton Ball				
Marble				
Toothpick				
Paper Clip				

Unit E • Chapter 1   Assessment Guide AG 75

PERFORMANCE TASK

Teacher's Directions

Mix and See

Materials marbles, toothpicks, cotton balls, paper clips, water, paper, clear plastic containers

Time 20–30 minutes

Suggested Grouping pairs

Science Processes predict, record data

Preparation Hints Set up one area where children can come to get water. Assemble other materials.

Introduce the Task Elicit the different things that can happen when objects are put into water (for example, life preservers float; anchors sink; paper things may lose their shape). Tell children that they will make some predictions about what will happen to some things when they put them into water. Distribute Performance Task sheets and materials. Ask children to read the directions silently. Then have volunteers explain the directions so that children can confirm or correct their understanding.

Promote Discussion When children finish, ask them to share their task results with a partner. Have children tell whether or not their predictions were correct.

Scoring Rubric

Performance Indicators

____ Writes a prediction about what will happen to the four items.

____ Follows through on directions for immersing the four items.

____ Records results accurately.

____ Articulates clearly both predictions and results of immersing items.

Observations and Rubric Score

3	2	1	0

AG 76 **Assessment Guide** Unit E • Chapter 1

Name _____
Date _____

 Chapter Assessment

Making Sound

Part I   Vocabulary

Write the letter of the best choice.

___ 1. Something used to make music

___ 2. Something you hear

___ 3. How high or low a sound is

___ 4. Moves back and forth very fast

A pitch
B sound
C vibrates
D musical instrument

Part II   Science Concepts and Understanding

Circle the best answer to each question.

5. What must a rubber band do to make sound?

   stretch   vibrate

6. What word describes a dog that has a loud, low bark?

   big   small

Unit E • Chapter 2   (page 1 of 4)   Assessment Guide   AG 77

Name _____

7. Which bell makes a higher sound?
　　　small bell　　big bell

8. A whistle makes a sound with a high pitch. How fast do its parts vibrate?
　　　fast　　　　slow

9. Which one often makes a softer sound?
　　　kitten　　　cat

10. Which makes a louder sound?
　　　shout　　　whisper

11. Draw a musical instrument you pluck to make a sound.

Name _____

12. Draw a musical instrument you beat to make sound.

```
┌─────────────────────────────────────┐
│                                     │
│                                     │
│                                     │
└─────────────────────────────────────┘
```

Part III Process Skills Application

Process skills: investigate, use numbers, form a hypothesis

Write the letter that best describes the amount of water in each bottle.

13. ___

14. ___

15. ___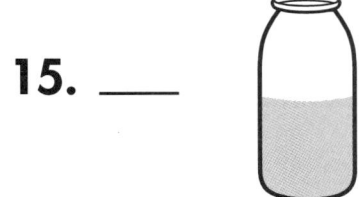

A. about $\frac{1}{4}$ cup

B. about $\frac{1}{2}$ cup

C. about 1 cup

Name _____

16. Circle the letter for the bottle that makes the highest sound when you blow across its top.

A   **B**   **C**

17. Draw a small bell. Then draw one that is a little larger and one that is a lot larger.

18. Color the bell that makes the lowest sound.

Name _____ Date _____

Sound Test

Materials

rubber bands (two different widths)   box lid   pencil   paper

1. Stretch a thin and a wide rubber band across the lid of a box.
2. Predict which rubber band will make the highest sound and which will make the loudest sound.
3. Pluck each rubber band and compare the sounds they make.
4. On the chart below, record what kind of sound each one makes.

Rubber Bands	Sound	
	Loud-Soft	High-Low
1. thin		
2. wide		

5. Compare what you predicted with what you found out.

Unit E • Chapter 2

Teacher's Directions

Sound Test

PERFORMANCE TASK

Materials — rubber bands (two different widths), box lid, pencil, paper

Time — 20–30 minutes

Suggested Grouping — individuals, pairs, or small groups

Science Processes — predict, investigate, compare

Preparation Hints — Group the rubber bands by width. Have a sample lid for the children to observe. Have the other materials ready.

Introduce the Task — Hold up the sample lid and pluck one rubber band. Ask children to describe the sound. Using this experience, encourage children to predict the characteristics of the sounds from the other rubber bands.

Promote Discussion — Have children compare their predictions with their results and tell what they learned from the Sound Test.

Scoring Rubric

Performance Indicators

_____ Makes a prediction relating rubber band width and pitch.

_____ Makes a prediction relating rubber band width and loudness.

_____ Compares the prediction with the results.

_____ Explains what was learned from the investigation.

Observations and Rubric Score

| 3 | 2 | 1 | 0 |

AG 82 Assessment Guide — Unit E • Chapter 2

Name _____
Date _____

Matter and Energy

Circle the letter of the best answer.

1. What kind of matter does this picture show?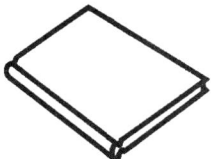

   A solid **B** liquid **C** gas

2. Which of these pictures shows a liquid?

   F

   G

   H

3. Which word tells about this picture?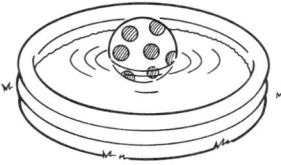

   A sink **B** float **C** dissolve

Unit E   Assessment Guide   AG 83

Name _____

4. Which solid would dissolve in a liquid?

   F a sugar cube   **G** a block of wood   **H** a rock

5. What is air made of?

   A gases   **B** liquids   **C** solids

6. Which word tells what happened in these two pictures?

   F dissolve   **G** vibrate   **H** change

7. Which word tells about something you can hear?

   A matter   **B** sound   **C** dissolve

8. Which of these would make a sound with a high pitch?

   F a large gong

   G a large bass drum

   H a set of small bell chimes

Name _____

9. Which picture shows a musical instrument?

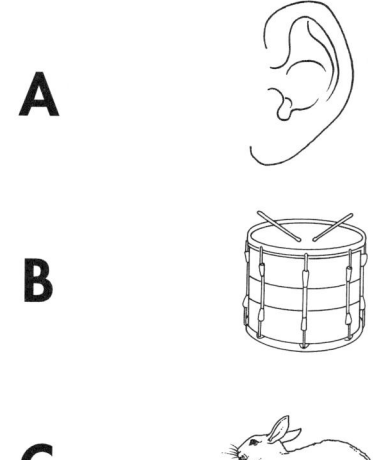

A

B

C

10. What must a musical instrument do to make a sound?

    F vibrate   **G** pitch   **H** change

Circle the word that completes the sentence.

11. You, your pencil, and a cup of water are all _____.

    matter   solids   nonliving things

Unit E

Name _____

12. Matter that keeps its shape is a _____.

   liquid   **solid**   **gas**

13. A _____ is a kind of matter that takes the shape of its container.

   liquid   **solid**   **gas**

Write the answer in the blank.

14. A ringing bell, a friend talking, and thunder are all _____.

15. A musical instrument that vibrates very _____ makes a high pitched sound.

Name _____
Date _____

Pushes and Pulls

Part 1 Vocabulary

Draw a line to match each word with its picture.

1. push •   •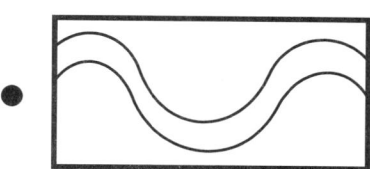

2. pull •   •

3. curve •   •

4. wheel •   •

5. speed •   •

Circle the word that completes the sentence.

6. A push or a pull is a

    surface   **force**   **block**

Name _____

7. Moving from one place to another is called

    motion   **ramp**   **smooth**

8. The top or outside of something is called its

    friction   **push**   **surface**

9. A force that makes it harder to move things is

    pull   **speed**   **friction**

Part II   Science Concepts and Understanding

10. Circle the things that are being pushed.

Name _____

11. Put an **X** under the animal that is moving faster.

_____   _____

Circle the letter of the correct answer.

12. A path that changes directions is a

    A miss   **B** curve   **C** hit

13. A ball rolls farther on a

    F rough surface
    G smooth surface
    H bumpy surface

14. Circle the surface that has more friction.

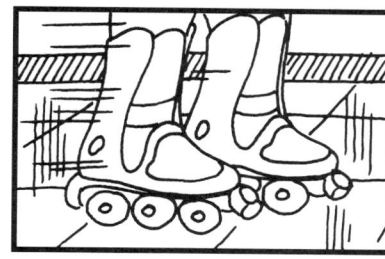   

Name _____

Part III Process Skills Application

Process skills: measure, draw a conclusion

15. Look at the pictures.
Then complete the chart.

Meters Moved in One Minute

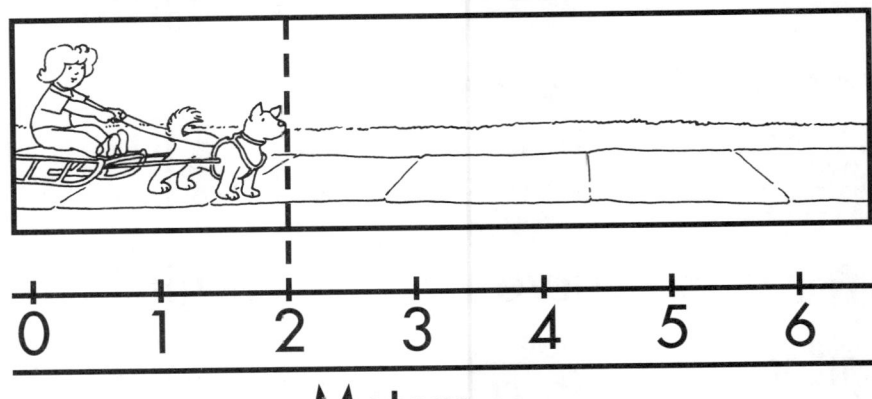

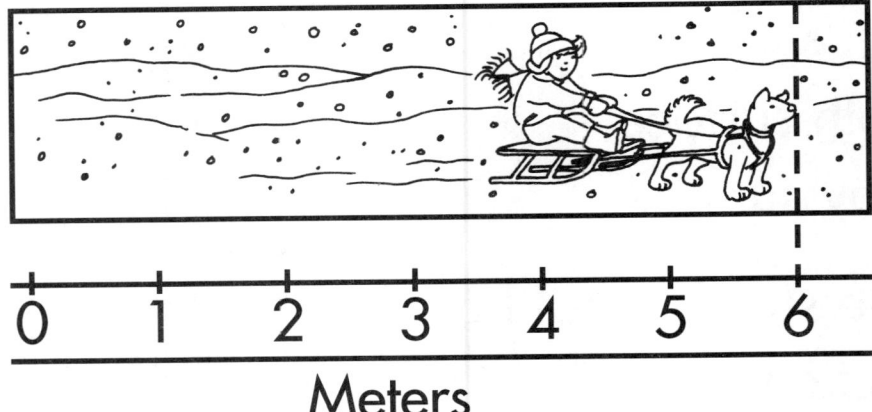

Meters Moved in One Minute

On the sidewalk	
On the snow	

Unit F • Chapter 1

Name _____ Date _____

Game of Pushes

Materials: box lid, crayons or markers, bottle cap, clay, craft stick

1. Make your box lid look like a gameboard as you see in the drawing.

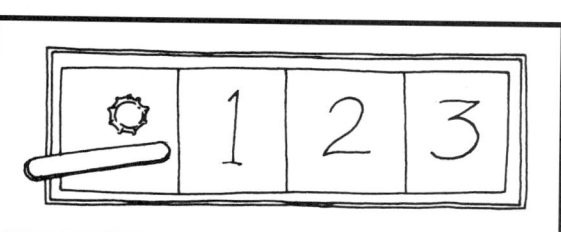

2. Use the craft stick to push the bottle cap and see where it stops. What score did you make?

3. See how many points you can score with three pushes.

4. Add a piece of clay to the bottom of the bottle cap. Try to push it again.

5. Describe the force needed to move the bottle cap with and without clay.

PERFORMANCE TASK

Teacher's Directions

Game of Pushes

Materials shoe box lids, crayons or markers, bottle caps, clay, craft sticks

Time 20–30 minutes

Suggested Grouping individuals and small groups

Science Processes use a model

Preparation Hints You can substitute drawing paper for box lids, checkers or small wads of paper for bottle caps, and rulers or pencils for craft sticks. Prepare a sample gameboard.

Introduce the Task On the sample gameboard, pretend to push a bottle cap, but stop just before you do so. Ask children to predict which way the bottle cap will go. Follow through with your push so children can see if they were right. Then ask volunteers to pretend to push and classmates to predict where the bottle cap will go. Distribute the Performance Task sheets, and ask children to read the directions silently. Distribute the remaining materials. Ask volunteers to describe what they will do to complete the task.

Promote Discussion Ask children to report their scores and their experience moving the bottle cap with and without clay stuck to it. What do children think accounted for the difference? (The clay produced friction that made the bottle cap hard to move.)

Scoring Rubric

Performance Indicators

_____ Makes a gameboard with the numbers 1, 2, and 3.
_____ Pushes bottle cap using craft stick.
_____ Records the number of points scored.
_____ Compares the amount of force needed to move the bottle cap with and without clay stuck to it.

Observations and Rubric Score

| 3 | 2 | 1 | 0 |

AG 92 **Assessment Guide**   Unit F • Chapter 1

Name _____
Date _____

Magnets

Part 1   Vocabulary

Draw a line from the word to the picture it goes with.

1. poles •

2. repel •

3. attract •

    • [S ↔ S]

    • [N S]

    • [→N S←]

Circle the best answer.

4. A piece of iron that can pull things is a ___.

   rock   **stone**   **magnet**

5. A magnet's ___ is how strongly it pulls.

   pole   **strength**   **plan**

6. A ___ can pass through paper.

   magnetic force   **natural force**   **small force**

Unit F • Chapter 2

Name _____

7. A magnet can ___ the things it attracts.

magnetize   **repel**   **push**

Part II Science Concepts and Understanding

8. Circle things a magnet attracts.

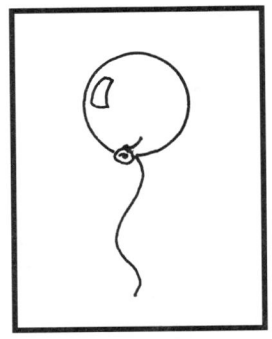   

9. Which pole will attract the *S* pole of another magnet? Put an *X* on it.

10. Put an *X* on the pole that will repel the *S* pole of another magnet.

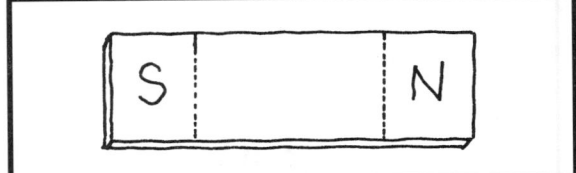

Name _____

11. Write the word that completes *both* sentences.

All magnets have ___ in them.

Magnets attract objects that are made of ___.

_____

Write the letter of the best answer.

___ **12.** Where is a magnet's pull the strongest?
    A at the poles
    B in the middle
    C above the magnet

___ **13.** What can you make a magnet from?
    F a crayon
    G a book
    H a paper clip

___ **14.** What kind of magnet is found in the ground?
    A a gem stone
    B a lodestone
    C a diamond

Name _____

Part III Process Skills Application

Process skills: infer, investigate

15. Put an **X** by the sentence that tells what you can infer from this picture.

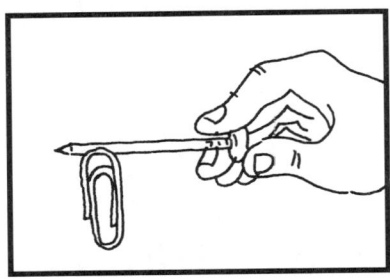

___ The nail repels the paper clip.

___ The nail has been magnetized.

16. You plan to investigate whether you can make a magnet out of a nail. Write **1**, **2**, and **3** to show the order of the steps you would take.

___ See if the nail will pull paper clips.

___ Touch the nail to the paper clips again to see if it will pull them.

___ Stroke the nail with a magnet ten times in the same direction.

Name _____ Date _____

Comparing Magnet Strength

Materials

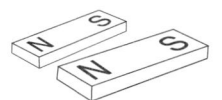   

two magnets   paper clips   masking tape   marker

1. Put a small piece of tape near the middle of each magnet. Write **A** on one piece of tape and **B** on the other.

2. How can you find out which magnet is stronger? Plan an investigation using the two magnets and some paper clips. Then follow your plan.

3. Draw a picture of your investigation. Put a star beside the stronger magnet in your picture.

4. Share with classmates what you found out.

PERFORMANCE TASK

Teacher's Directions

Comparing Magnet Strength

Materials Performance Task sheets, a variety of magnets—two different ones for each pair of children, paper clips, masking tape, markers

Time 20–30 minutes

Suggested Grouping pairs or small groups

Science Processes investigate, gather data, record

Preparation Hints Each pair of children will need 10 to 20 paper clips, depending on the size and strength of the magnets.

Introduce the Task Ask three children to select one magnet each from the assortment you have gathered. Then ask these children to demonstrate that what they selected *is* a magnet. Have them show how it picks up or attaches itself to metal objects. Brainstorm with children how they might investigate which of the three magnets is the strongest. Have children compare how well each attracts the same metal object. Distribute the Performance Task sheets. Ask one volunteer to read the directions aloud. Ask other children to explain what they will be doing.

Promote Discussion When children finish, have the partners join others in a small group to compare their work. Have one partner in each pair describe the investigation they did and its outcome. Ask the groups to decide which of the magnets used by its members was stronger and how they know.

Scoring Rubric

Performance Indicators

_____ Plans an investigation to determine which magnet is stronger.
_____ Follows the investigation plan.
_____ Draws a picture of the investigation.
_____ Uses the picture to explain the investigation and its outcome to others.

Observations and Rubric Score

| 3 | 2 | 1 | 0 |

Name _____

Date _____

Unit Assessment

Forces

Circle the letter of the best answer.

1. Which word tells about a kind of a force?

    A straight   **B** push   **C** surface

2. Which is a change in direction?

    F up and down   **G** curve   **H** friction

3. Which of these words tells a way things can move?

    A straight   **B** friction   **C** magnet

4. Which word tells how an object moves from one place to another?

    F poles   **G** surface   **H** motion

5. Which of these surfaces has the least amount of friction?

    A wood   **B** carpet   **C** ice

Unit F   (page 1 of 4)   Assessment Guide   AG 99

Name _____

6. Which word tells about this picture?

   F force   **G** wheel   **H** push

7. What do all magnets attract?

   A motion   **B** iron   **C** friction

8. Which magnet has the most strength?

F
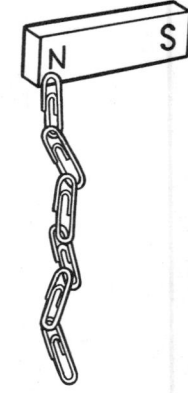

G
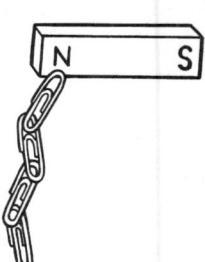

H

AG 100 Assessment Guide   (page 2 of 4)   **Unit F**

Name _____

9. Which picture shows two magnets that will repel each other?

A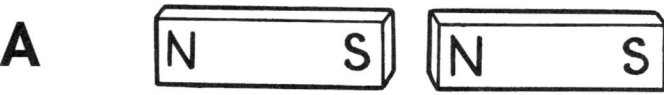

B

C [N   S][S   N]

10. Which one of these can you magnetize?

   F a glass of water

   G an iron nail

   H a wooden wheel

Circle the word that completes the sentence.

11. How quickly something moves is called its _____.

   friction   **push**   **speed**

Name _____

12. Magnetic _____ can pull through paper.

motion **force** **friction**

13. A magnetic force is strongest when two magnets are _____.

close together **far apart** **in a liquid**

Write the answer in the blank.

14. A force is a push or a _____.

15. The two places on a magnet where the pulling force is the greatest are called the _____.

Unit A • Chapter 1

Living and Nonliving Things

Part I Vocabulary 4 points each

Circle the word that answers the question.

1. What do we call hearing, sight, touch, smell, and taste?

    ears   hands   (senses)

Circle the word that names the pictures.

2. (living)   nonliving

3. living   (nonliving)

Part II Science Concepts and Understanding

Draw a line from each sense to the child using it. 6 points each

4. sight
5. hearing
6. touch
7. taste
8. smell

---

9. Circle each word that tells what these living things need.

    (water) food   (air) (water)

10. Circle each word that tells what these living things do.

    (grows) sees   (changes) (hears)

11. Circle the nonliving thing.

    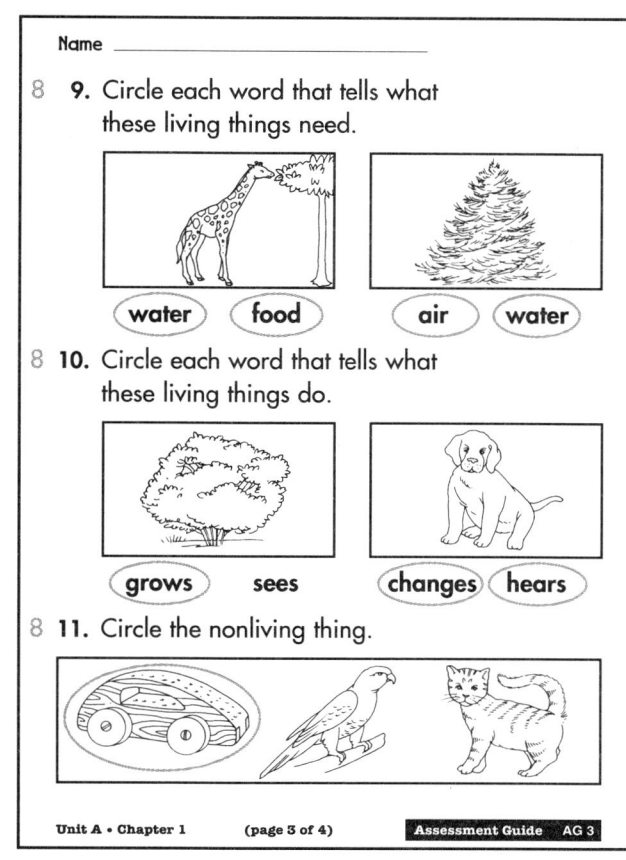

Part III Process Skills Application 17 points each

Process skills: observe, compare

12. Write **g** under the thing that grows.

    g   ___

13. Write **c** under the thing that changes.

    ___   c

Answer Key

Unit A • Chapter 2

All About Plants

Part I Vocabulary 4 points each

Circle the word or words that complete each sentence.

1. Most plants grow from a

    flower   stem   (seed)

2. The outside of a seed is its

    stem   (seed coat)   flower

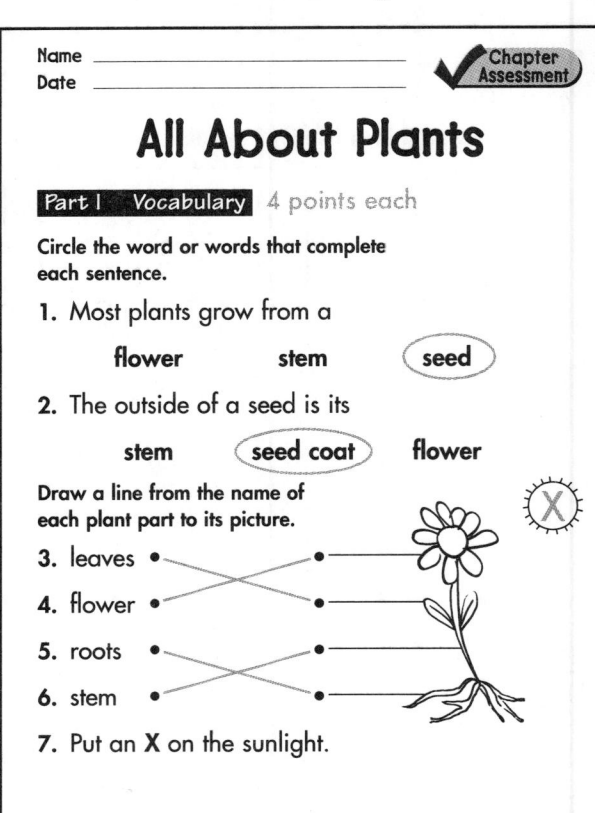

3. leaves
4. flower
5. roots
6. stem

7. Put an **X** on the sunlight.

Part II Science Concepts and Understanding 8 points each

We eat parts of some plants.

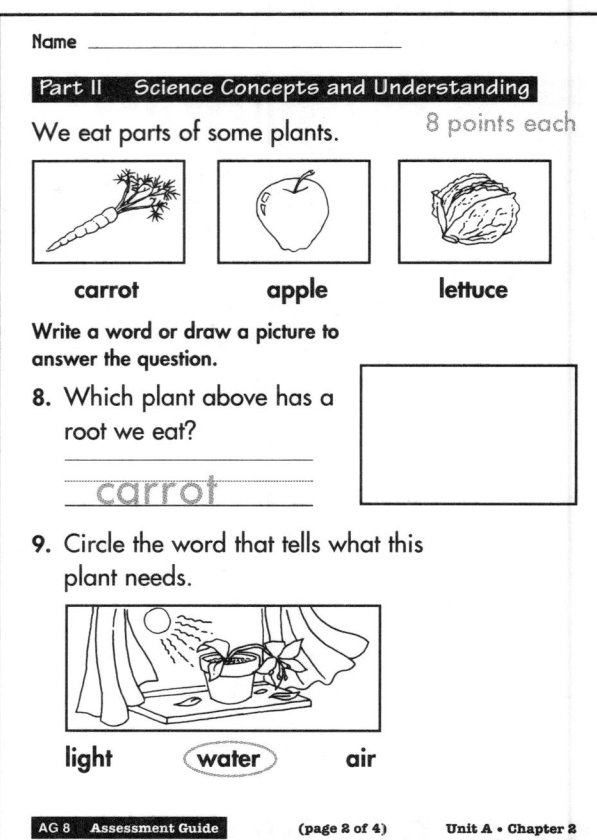

carrot   apple   lettuce

Write a word or draw a picture to answer the question.

8. Which plant above has a root we eat?

    carrot

9. Circle the word that tells what this plant needs.

    light   (water)   air

---

10. Circle what the flowers under the tree need.

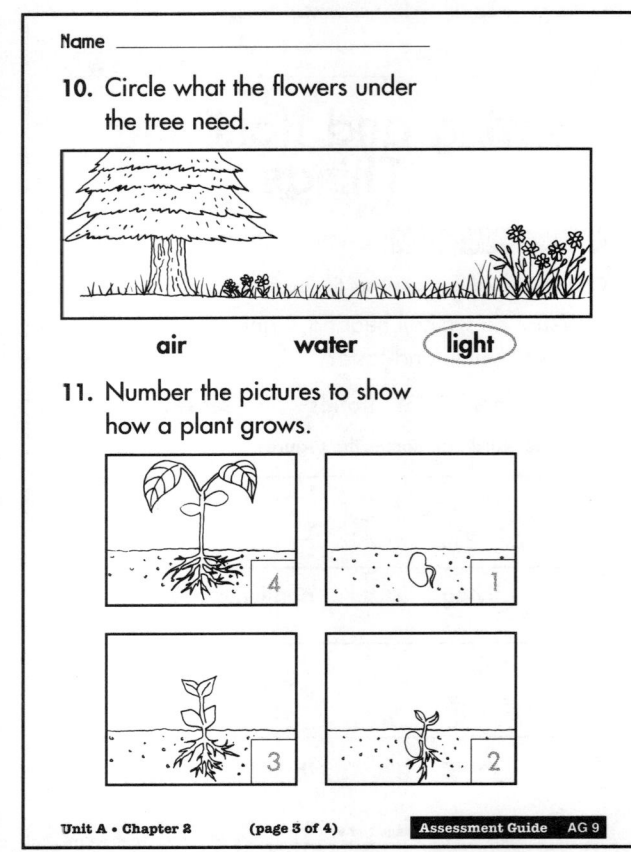

air   water   (light)

11. Number the pictures to show how a plant grows.

    [4] [1]
    [3] [2]

Part III Process Skills Application 20 points each

Process skills: observe, compare

12. Put an **X** under the plant whose seed was planted first.

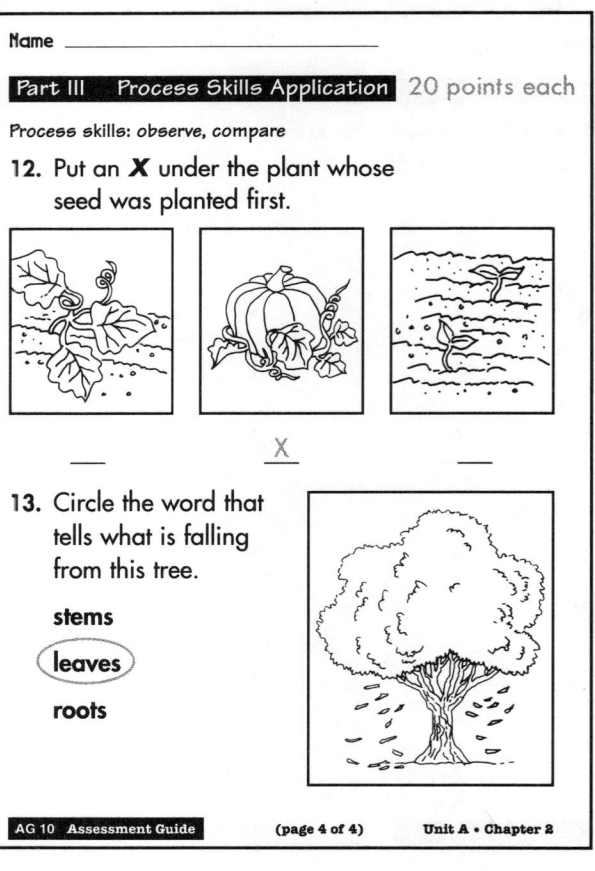

    ___   X   ___

13. Circle the word that tells what is falling from this tree.

    stems
    (leaves)
    roots

AG 104 Assessment Guide   **Answer Key**

Unit A • Chapter 3

All About Animals

Part I   Vocabulary — 4 points each

Draw a line from each word to the picture that matches it.

1. mammal
2. amphibian
3. reptile
4. gills
5. tadpole
6. insect
7. pupa
8. hatch
9. larva

(page 1 of 4)

Part II   Science Concepts and Understanding

5 points each

10. Circle what all animals need.

    wings   (food)   fins

11. Circle what helps some animals get air.

    feet   fur   (noses)

12. Circle the animal that builds a nest.

    (bird is circled)

13. Put an X on the part of the animal that helps it get water.

    (X on elephant's trunk)

(page 2 of 4)

---

14. Circle the word that tells what is in the picture.

    (reptiles)   mammals

15. Circle something that only birds have.

    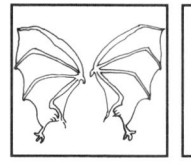  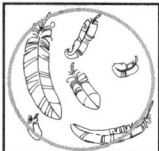

16. Circle something that only mammals have.

    feet   (fur)   wings

(page 3 of 4)

Part III   Process Skills Application

Process Skills: sequence, classify

8 17. Number the pictures to show how a butterfly grows.

   4   1
   2   3

Circle the word to classify each animal.

7 18. (bee)	has six legs	mammal / (insect)
7 19. (frog)	has wet skin	bird / (amphibian)
7 20. (fish)	has gills	reptile / (fish)

(page 4 of 4)

Answer Key

AG 105 Assessment Guide

Unit A

Plants and Animals All Around
Circle the correct answer. 5 points each

1. Which body part do you use for hearing?
   eye   mouth   (ear)

2. What sense tells you how something looks?
   smell   taste   (sight)

3. Which is nonliving?

4. Where do plant seeds come from?

5. A plant's roots take in _____.
   soil   (water)   sunlight

6. What part makes food for a plant?

7. What do you plant to grow new plants?
   eggs   flowers   (seeds)

8. What do plants need to live?
   (water)   wind   rocks

9. Plants need air and _____ to make food.
   soil   (sunlight)   people

10. Animals need food, water, air, and a place to _____.
    (live)   eat   run

11. What do fish use to breathe?
    nose   lungs   (gills)

12. Which is a mammal?
13. Which is an amphibian?

14. Which is an insect?
    (ant)   frog   salamander

15. Snakes are a type of _____.
    bird   mammal   (reptile)

16. Chicks _____ out of eggs.
    eat   taste   (hatch)

17. Which picture shows an animal caring for its young?

18. Which grows inside a pupa?
      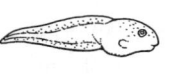

19. What is another word for a caterpillar?
    (larva)   butterfly   tadpole

20. A young frog is a _____.
    chick   (tadpole)   larva

Answer Key

Unit B • Chapter 1

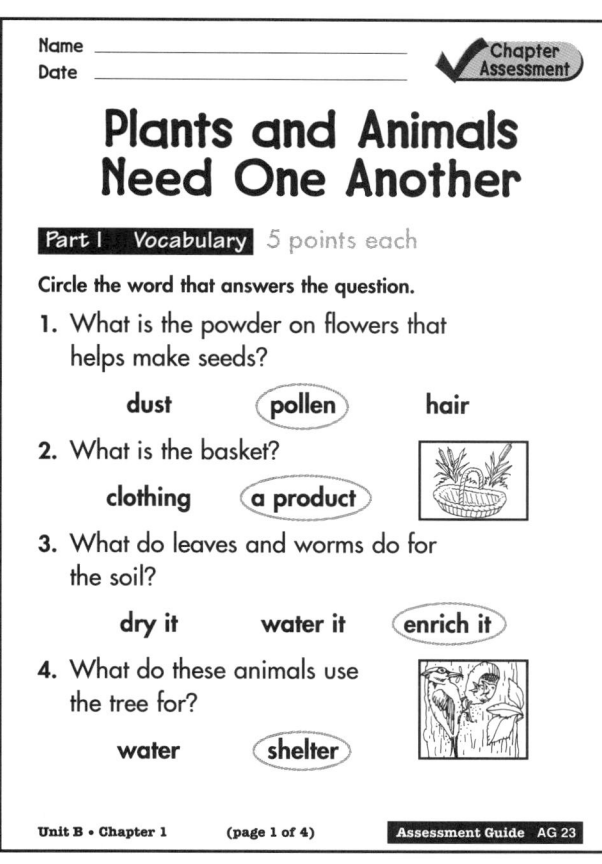

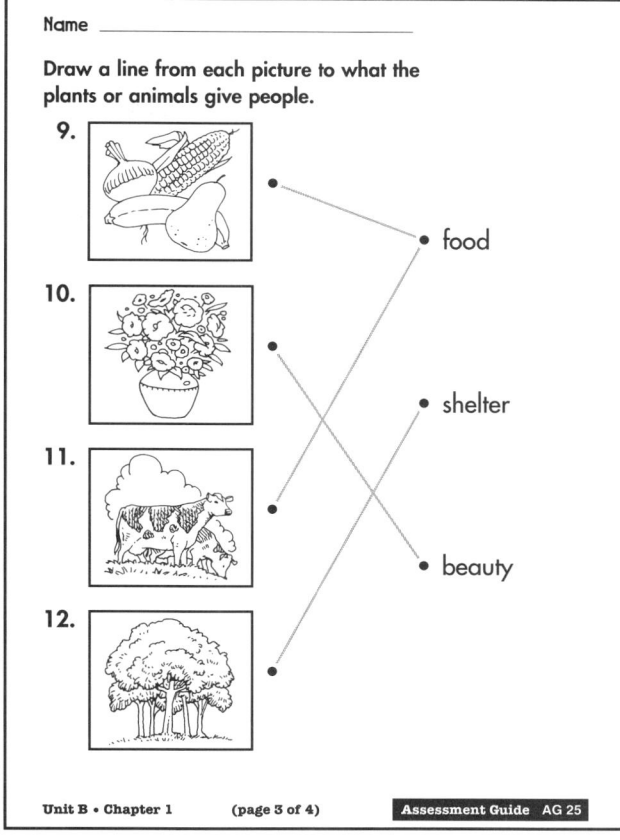

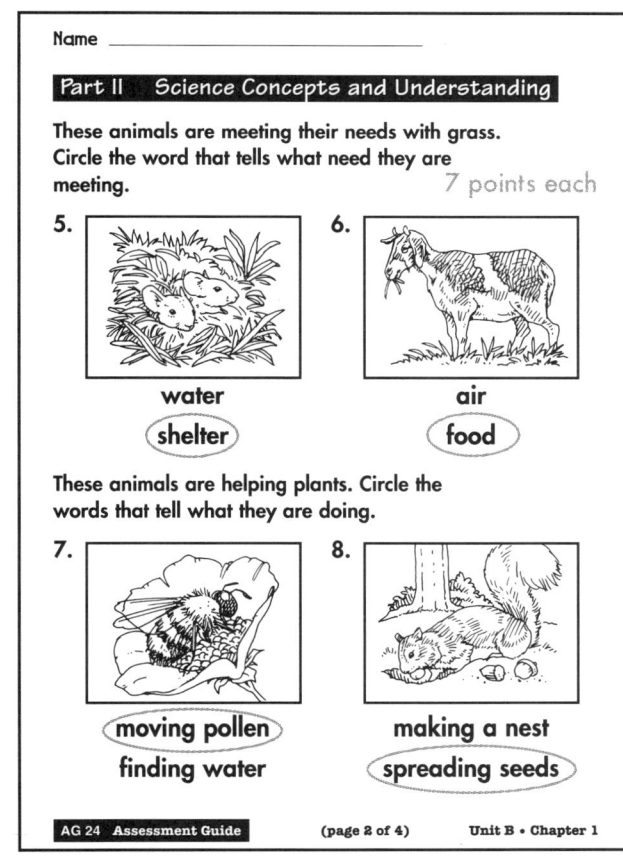

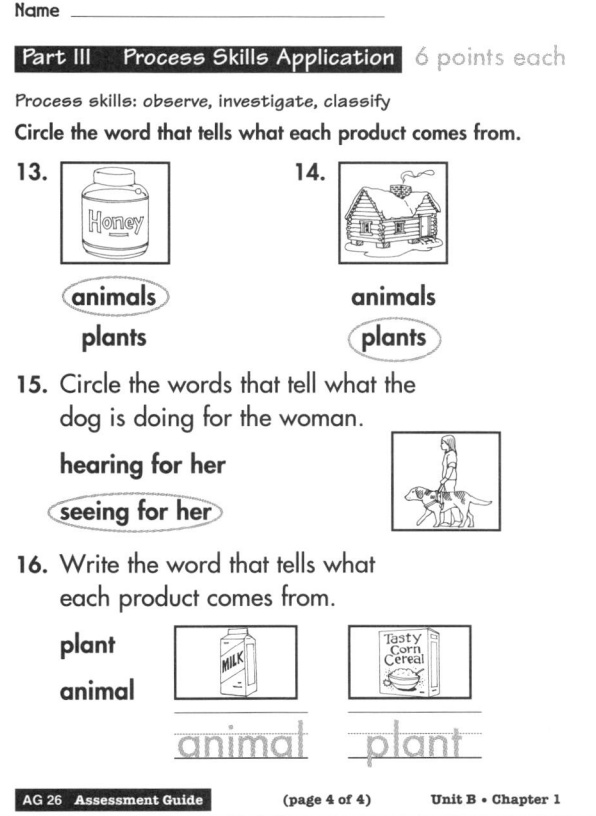

Answer Key

AG 107 Assessment Guide

Unit B • Chapter 2

A Place to Live

Part I Vocabulary 5 points each

Draw a line to the word or words that complete each sentence.

1. A dry place that gets a lot of sunlight and very little rain is a — **desert**
2. A place where the soil is moist and many trees grow is a — **forest**
3. A place that is wet all year and has many trees is a — **rain forest**
4. A large body of salt water is an — **ocean**
5. Seaweed is a kind of — **algae**

Part II Science Concepts and Understanding

Circle the answer to each question.   6 points each

6. What helps these plants grow in the forest?
   - (moist soil)
   - dry soil

7. What do these animals find in the forest?
   - (shelter)
   - seaweed

8. What can these desert plants hold in their leaves and stems?
   - soil
   - (water)

Circle the words or picture to answer each question.

9. Where do some desert animals get water?
   - from oceans
   - (from plants)

10. Which animal lives in the middle level of the rain forest?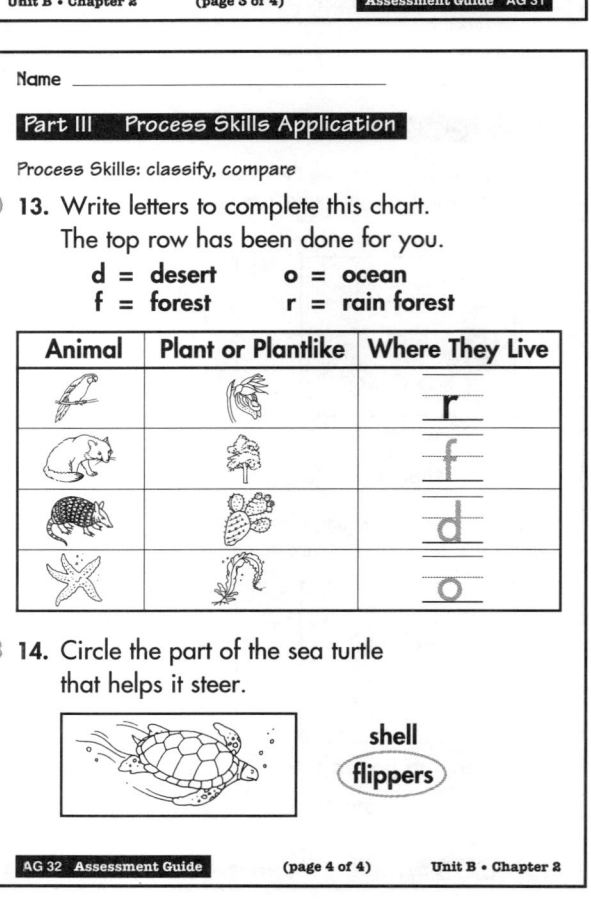

11. What covers more than half of Earth?
    - land
    - (oceans)

12. What do plants in the middle level of the rain forest get?
    - cold
    - (light)

Part III Process Skills Application

Process Skills: classify, compare

20 13. Write letters to complete this chart. The top row has been done for you.

d = desert   o = ocean
f = forest   r = rain forest

Animal	Plant or Plantlike	Where They Live
		r
		f
		d
		o

13 14. Circle the part of the sea turtle that helps it steer.
   - shell
   - (flippers)

Answer Key

Unit B

Name _____
Date _____

Living Together

Circle the correct answer. 6 points each

1. Which picture shows an animal using shelter?

2. Which animal eats both plants and animals?

   cow   rabbit   (raccoon)

3. Which animal is doing something that helps plants?

---

4. Which product is made from an animal?

   cotton balls   (wool sweater)   peanut butter

5. Where would you find many trees?

   desert   (forest)   ocean

6. Which would forest animals eat?

7. Which animal could live in the desert?

---

8. Which word tells about a desert?

   wet   (dry)   shady

9. Where do orchids grow in a rain forest?

   forest floor   (halfway up the trees)   top of the canopy

10. What word goes with this picture?

   desert   (ocean)   rain forest

Circle the word or words that belong in the blank. 8 points each

11. Worms can _____ the soil.

    destroy   (enrich)   water

12. A butterfly can help plants by carrying _____.

    seeds   flowers   (pollen)

13. Paper is a _____ made from plants.

    stage   leaf   (product)

14. A _____ is a warm, wet place with many trees.

    (rain forest)   ocean   desert

15. Seaweed is a type of _____.

    tree   animal   (algae)

Answer Key

Unit C • Chapter 1

Name _____
Date _____

Chapter Assessment

Earth's Land

Part I Vocabulary 4 points each

Circle the word that answers each question.

1. What is a hard, nonliving thing?

    (rock)   tree

2. What is made of very tiny pieces of rock?

    soil   (sand)

3. What are bones and imprints of animals that lived long ago?

    seashells   (fossils)

4. What word tells that a kind of plant or animal is gone forever?

    asleep   (extinct)

Unit C • Chapter 1   (page 1 of 4)   Assessment Guide AG 39

Name _____

Part II Science Concepts and Understanding

Circle the letter next to the word that completes each sentence. 6 points each

5. One way to sort rocks is by their

    A smell   (B) color   C sound

6. Glass products are made from

    (F) sand   G water   H air

7. An imprint of an extinct plant is a

    A starfish   B rock   (C) fossil

8. What can people make from rocks?

    F   (G)   H

AG 40 Assessment Guide   (page 2 of 4)   Unit C • Chapter 1

Name _____

9. Draw something that people use sand to make.

> Drawings may include an object made of glass, a sand castle, or a sand candle.

10. Complete the chart. Write L for living and N for nonliving.

rock	N
child	L
sand	N
fossil	N

11. What could help a dead plant or dead animal become a fossil? _____
    Possible answer: sap or mud that gets hard

Unit C • Chapter 1   (page 3 of 4)   Assessment Guide AG 41

Name _____

Part III Process Skills Application

Process skills: compare, classify

18 12. Circle the words that tell about each of these things.

What Are They Like?			
rocks	(smooth)	(rough)	soft
fossils	hot	(old)	(hard)
sand	(bits of rock)	bits of plant	bits of glass

Draw a line to match each kind of fossil to something we learn from it. 6 points each

13. fossil bones • • kind of food the animal ate

14. fossil teeth • • how big the animal was

15. fossil cone • • where water covered the land

16. fossil shell • • kind of seeds the plant had

AG 42 Assessment Guide   (page 4 of 4)   Unit C • Chapter 1

AG 110 Assessment Guide   **Answer Key**

Unit C • Chapter 2

Our Natural Resources

Part I   Vocabulary   5 points each

Draw a line from the word to the place on the map that it names.

1. lake
2. river
3. stream

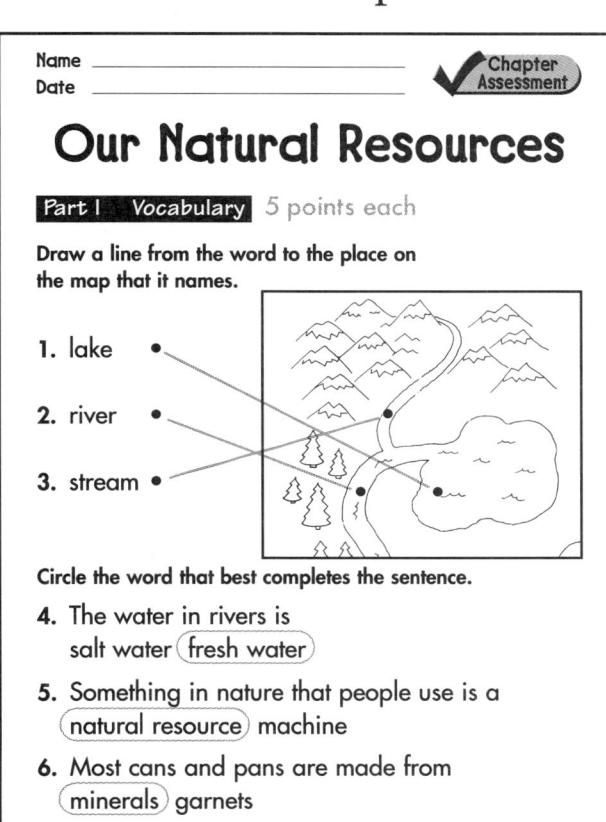

Circle the word that best completes the sentence.

4. The water in rivers is
   salt water   (fresh water)

5. Something in nature that people use is a
   (natural resource)   machine

6. Most cans and pans are made from
   (minerals)   garnets

---

7. What we feel when the wind blows is
   (air)   clouds

Draw a line to show what each word means. 5 points each

How We Help Save Natural Resources
8. reuse • — • use less of something
9. recycle • — • use something again
10. reduce • — • collect things so they can be made into new things

Part II   Science Concepts and Understanding

11. What do people recycle?
    A milk and soft drinks
    (B) cans and newspapers
    C sidewalks and streets

---

12. Circle the picture that does NOT show air moving.

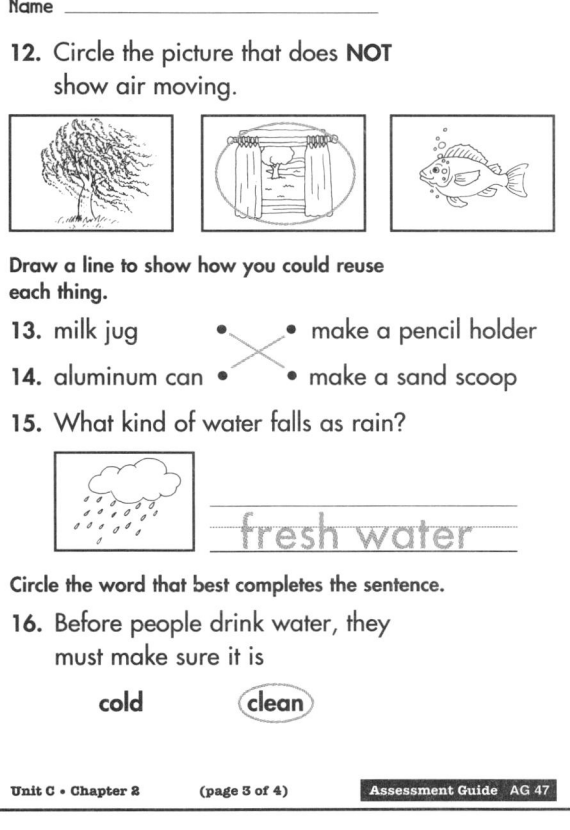

Draw a line to show how you could reuse each thing.

13. milk jug   • — • make a pencil holder
14. aluminum can   • — • make a sand scoop

15. What kind of water falls as rain?

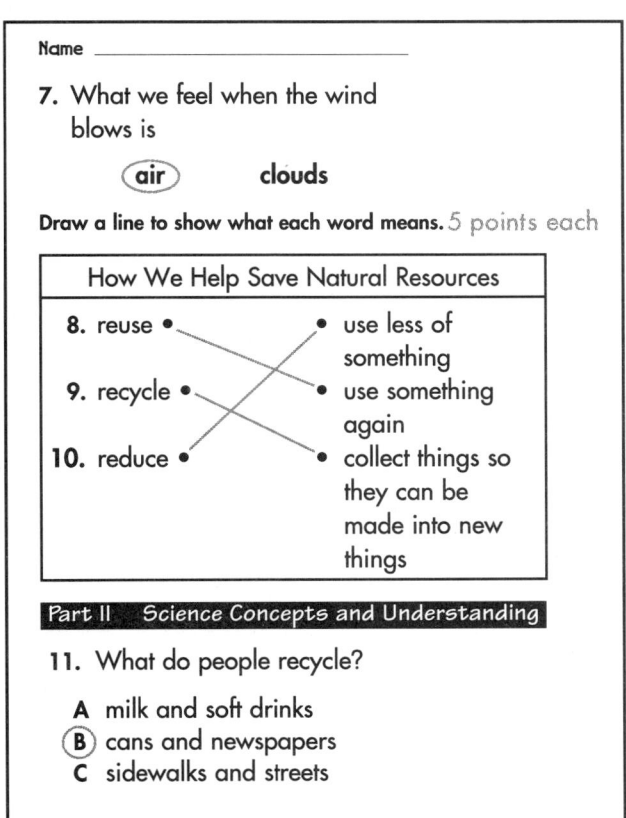 fresh water

Circle the word that best completes the sentence.

16. Before people drink water, they must make sure it is

    cold   (clean)

Part III   Process Skills Application   5 points each

Process skills: infer, communicate

17. Circle the word that tells what is in the bubbles.

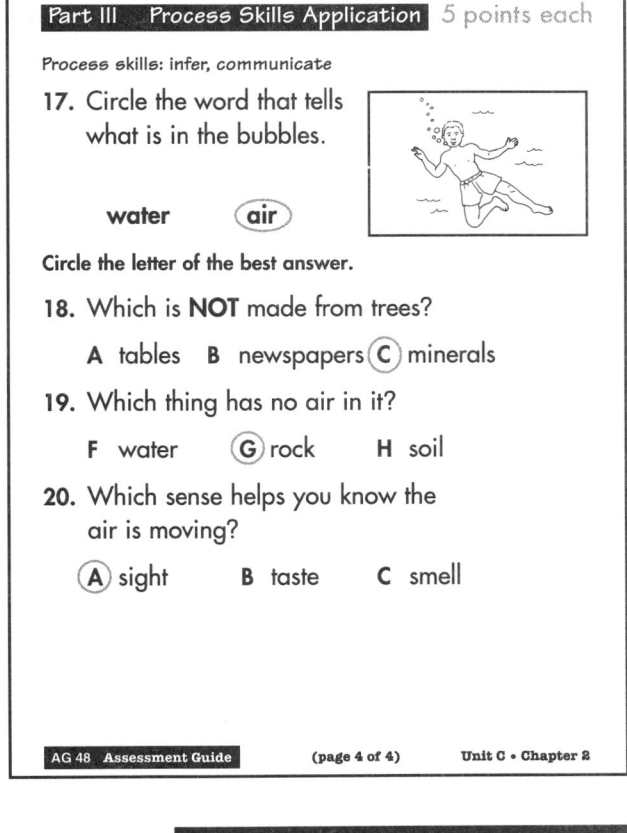

    water   (air)

Circle the letter of the best answer.

18. Which is NOT made from trees?
    A tables   B newspapers   (C) minerals

19. Which thing has no air in it?
    F water   (G) rock   H soil

20. Which sense helps you know the air is moving?
    (A) sight   B taste   C smell

Answer Key

AG 111 Assessment Guide

Unit C

About Our Earth
Circle the letter of the correct answer. 6 points each

1. What do you call tiny broken pieces of rock?
   A shells   (B) sand   C statues

2. Which word tells about rocks?
   F living   G extinct   (H) nonliving

3. What can be made from sand?
   A rock   (B) glass   C paper

4. Which word goes with this picture?

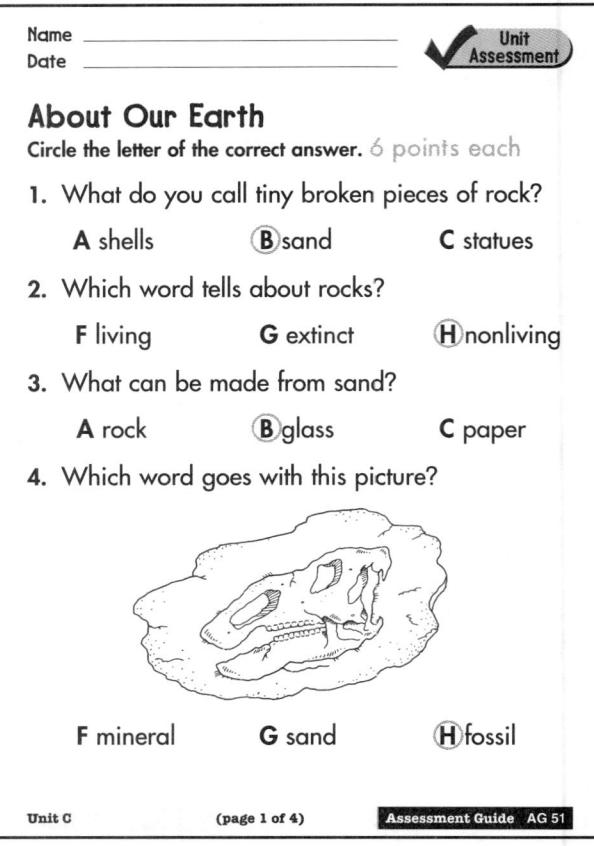

   F mineral   G sand   (H) fossil

---

8. Which picture shows a lake?
   (F)   G   H

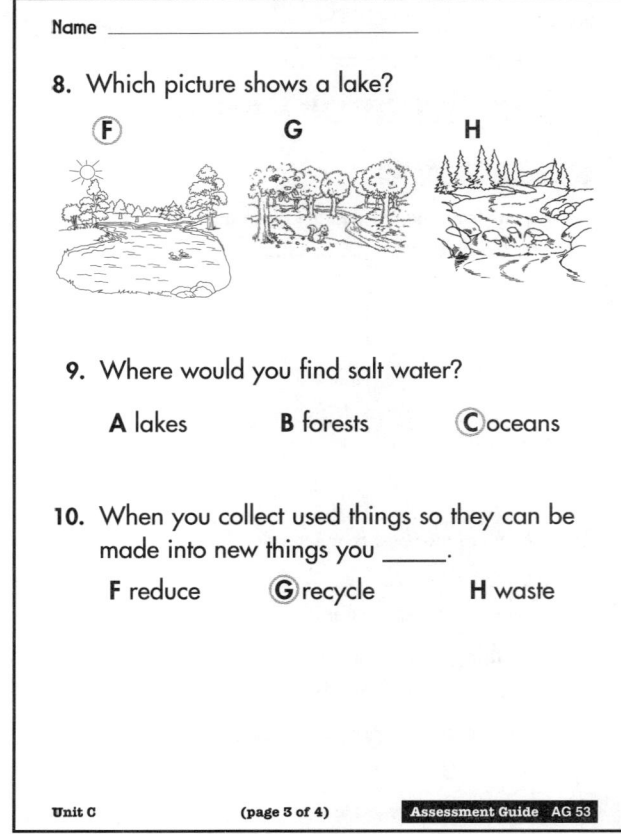

9. Where would you find salt water?
   A lakes   B forests   (C) oceans

10. When you collect used things so they can be made into new things you _____.
    F reduce   (G) recycle   H waste

---

5. Which word tells about a kind of plant that is no longer living?
   A natural   (B) extinct   C mineral

6. Which picture shows a natural resource?
   (F)   G   H

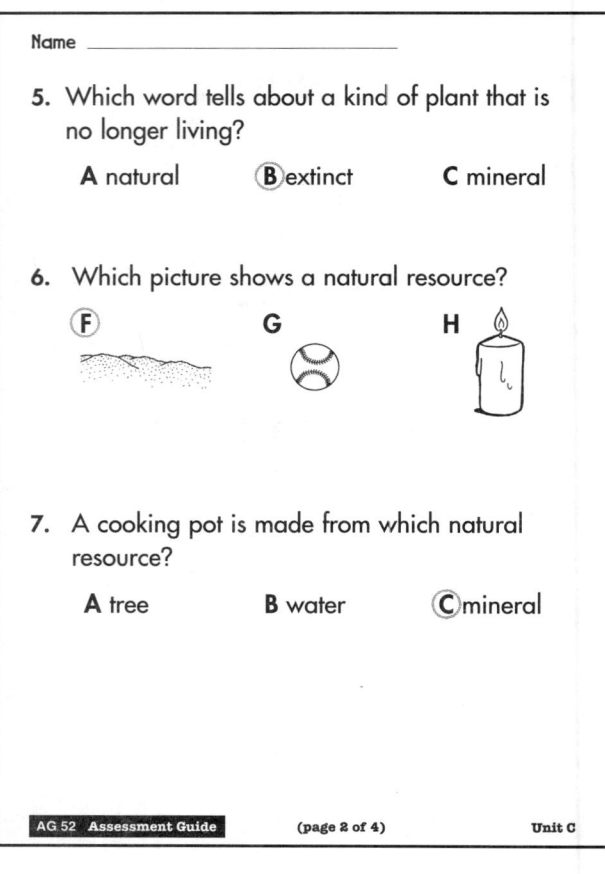

7. A cooking pot is made from which natural resource?
   A tree   B water   (C) mineral

Write the answer in the blank. 8 points each

| fresh water | air | fossils |
| reduce | natural resources | |

11. You can learn how plants and animals have changed by comparing them with __fossils__.

12. Minerals, water, and forests are kinds of __natural resources__.

13. A natural resource that you can't see, smell, or taste is __air__.

14. Water that is not salty is __fresh water__.

15. When you use a lunch box, you __reduce__ your use of paper.

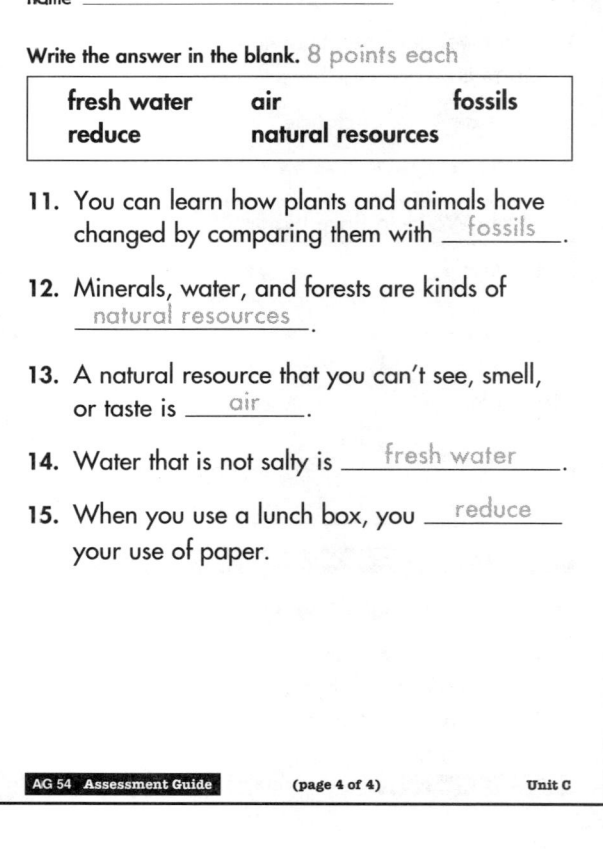

AG 112 Assessment Guide   **Answer Key**

Unit D • Chapter 1

Measuring Weather

Part I   Vocabulary   4 points each

Draw a line from each picture to a word or words for it.

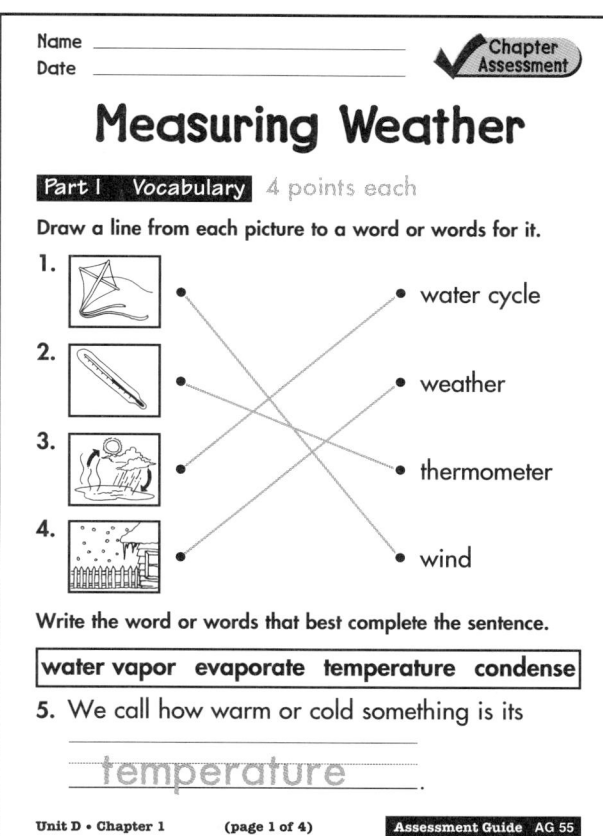

1. — wind
2. — thermometer
3. — water cycle
4. — weather

Write the word or words that best complete the sentence.

| water vapor   evaporate   temperature   condense |

5. We call how warm or cold something is its _temperature_.

---

6. Water that you can not see in the air is _water vapor_.

7. Warm air makes water _evaporate_.

8. Cooler air makes water vapor _condense_.

Part II   Science Concepts and Understanding

9. What does a meteorologist study?   6 points each

   weather

Circle the letter of the word that best completes the sentence.

10. At night, with no sunlight, the air feels

   A cloudy   (B) cooler   C warmer

---

11. Circle the letter of the city MOST likely to get rain.

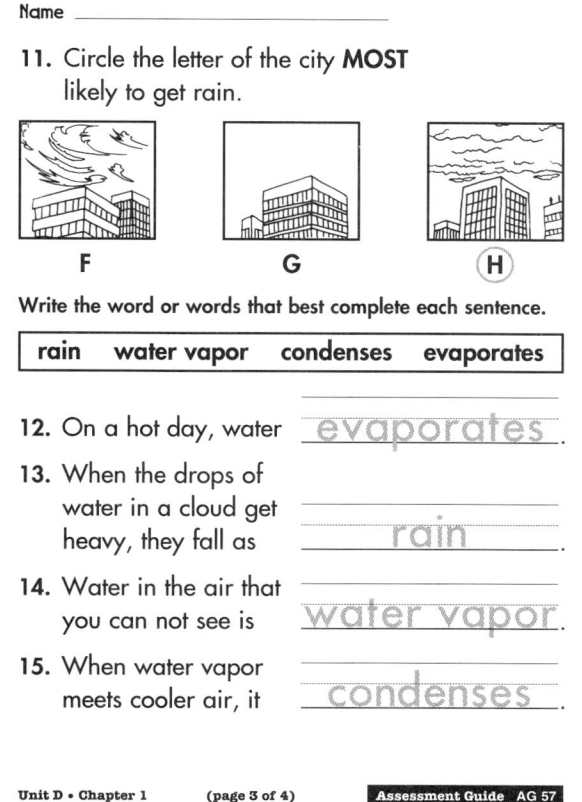

F   G   (H)

Write the word or words that best complete each sentence.

| rain   water vapor   condenses   evaporates |

12. On a hot day, water _evaporates_.

13. When the drops of water in a cloud get heavy, they fall as _rain_.

14. Water in the air that you can not see is _water vapor_.

15. When water vapor meets cooler air, it _condenses_.

Part III   Process Skills Application   13 points each

Process skills: observe, compare

16. Circle the picture that shows a windy day.

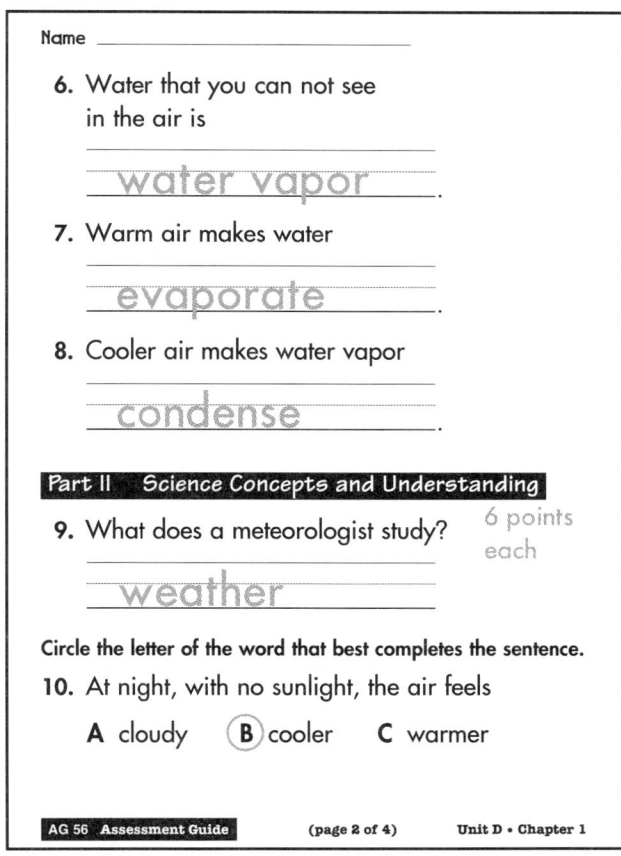

17. Circle the words that tell where the weather is warmer.

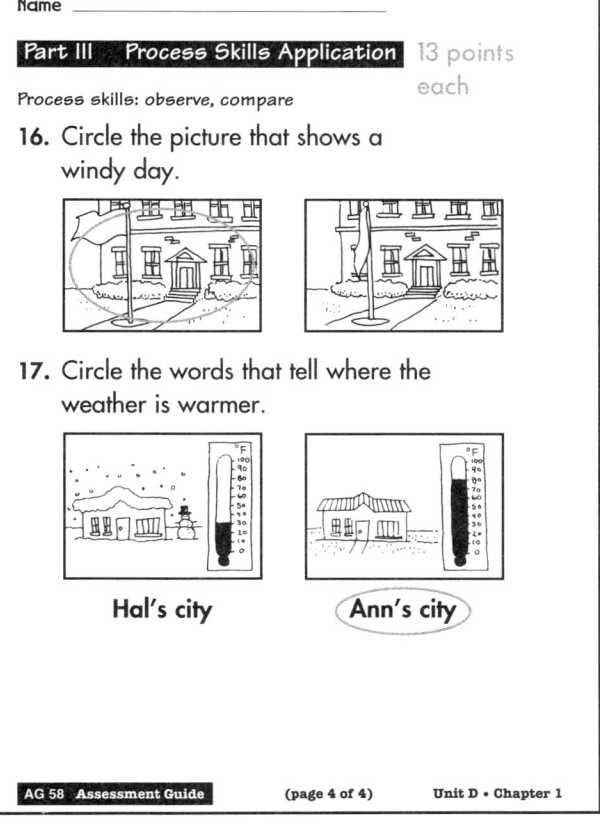

Hal's city   (Ann's city)

Answer Key   **AG 113 Assessment Guide**

Unit D • Chapter 2

Name _____
Date _____

Chapter Assessment

The Sky and the Seasons

Part I Vocabulary 4 points each

Write the letter of the word that belongs with each picture.

| A fall | B winter | C spring | D summer |

1. C 2. D 3. A 4. B

Write the letter of best choice.

C 5. Brightest object in the night sky
A 6. Far away objects that give off light
B 7. Makes the sky bright in the daytime
E 8. Spins like a top
D 9. A time of year

A stars
B sun
C moon
D season
E rotates

Name _____

Part II Science Concepts and Understanding

Circle the word that completes the sentence. 4 points each

10. We have day and night because Earth (rotates) stands still
11. Earth has four months (seasons)
12. Earth travels around the moon (sun)
13. The moon travels around (Earth) the stars
14. The sun is our closest (star) moon

Name _____

For Questions 15–17, draw a line from what a farmer does to the right season for it. 5 points each

What a Farmer Does   **The Season**

15. picks apples and pumpkins •   • summer
16. plants seeds   •   • spring
17. takes care of crops as they grow • • fall

18. In which season do we see plants beginning to come out of the ground?

spring

Name _____

Part III Process Skills Application 8 points each

Process Skills: order, predict, investigate

The graph below shows the hours of light in a day.

19. Put an **X** on the name of the season that has the most hours of daylight.

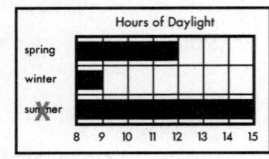

20. In which season will this squirrel look for what it is burying?

winter

21. Put an **X** by the best way to investigate what will grow from a seed.

   X Plant it. Put it near a window. Water it.
   __ Cut it in half. Observe.
   __ Try to find the seed in a book about plants.

Answer Key

Unit D

Weather, the Sky, and Seasons
Write the letter of the correct answer. 8 points each

__B__ 1. What would you use to measure temperature?

  A (measuring cup)   B (thermometer)   C (arrow)

__H__ 2. Which thermometer shows the warmest temperature?

  F   G   H

(page 1 of 4) — Assessment Guide AG 67

__C__ 3. Which picture shows part of the water cycle?

  A (tornado)   B (flag)   C (rain cloud)

__G__ 4. What is something you see in the sky at night?
  F sun   G moon   H Earth

__A__ 5. Where does Earth's heat and light come from?
  A the sun   B the wind   C the moon

__H__ 6. Which tells why Earth has night and day?
  F water cycle   G evaporates   H rotates

AG 68 Assessment Guide (page 2 of 4)

__B__ 7. When do most animals give birth to young?
  A winter   B spring   C summer

__G__ 8. What do children do in the summer?
  F rake leaves   G swim outdoors   H go sledding

__B__ 9. What happens in the fall?
  A snow falls   B leaves fall   C temperatures rise

__H__ 10. What happens to the water in a puddle on a sunny day?
  F It gets deeper.   G It goes into a lake.   H It goes into the air.

(page 3 of 4) — Assessment Guide AG 69

__A__ 11. Which picture shows winter?

  A   B   C

Write the answer in the blank. 3 points each

| water vapor | weather |
| wind | seasons |

12. Spring, summer, winter, and fall are all names of ___seasons___.

13. The words cloudy, snowy, or cold all tell about the ___weather___.

14. Water in the air that you can not see is ___water vapor___.

15. Moving air that helps to fly a kite is called ___wind___.

AG 70 Assessment Guide (page 4 of 4)

Answer Key AG 115 Assessment Guide

Unit E • Chapter 1

Investigate Matter

Part I Vocabulary 4 points each

Write the letter of the word that best completes the sentence.

A change	C gas	E liquid	G sink
B floats	D matter	F dissolve	H solid

The air that fills the tube is a **1.** C .
The tube keeps its shape, so it is a **2.** H .
The tube **3.** B on the top of a **4.** E .
The goggles **5.** G to the bottom.
Salt can **6.** F in water.
Everything in the picture is **7.** D .
You can **8.** A an object by bending it.

Part II Science Concepts and Understanding

Circle the letter of the best answer. 6 points each

9. How are these solids sorted?
   - (A) by shape
   - B by sound
   - C by color

10. What is a way to measure liquids?
    - F by color
    - G by shape
    - (H) by amount

11. Which object will float?
    - A an anchor
    - (B) a cork
    - C a ball of clay

12. What is inside a beach ball that helps it float?

    a gas

13. Which liquids do **NOT** mix?
    - F vinegar and water
    - (G) oil and water
    - H milk and water

Draw a line to what will happen.

14. If you fill a jar with water, • → it will take the shape of the jar.
15. If you fill a jar with marbles, • → they will keep their shape.
16. If you fill a jar with gas, • → it will fill up the space in the jar.

17. Write two ways to classify these objects.

by __shape__   by __size__

Part III Process Skills Application 7 points each

Process skills: collect and record data, draw conclusions

18. Put an **X** below the words that tell what does **NOT** mix.

warm water and cold water	warm water and ice cubes	oil and water
___	___	X

19. Look at the bottles. Make a tally mark for each bottle.

 A   B   C   D   E

Matter

	A	B	C	D	E	Total
Solid	l	l				2
Liquid			l		l	2
Gas	l	l	l	l	l	5

Answer Key

Unit E • Chapter 2

Name _____
Date _____

Chapter Assessment

Making Sound

Part I Vocabulary 4 points each

Write the letter of the best choice.

_D_ 1. Something used to make music
_B_ 2. Something you hear
_A_ 3. How high or low a sound is
_C_ 4. Moves back and forth very fast

A pitch
B sound
C vibrates
D musical instrument

Part II Science Concepts and Understanding

Circle the best answer to each question. 6 points each

5. What must a rubber band do to make sound?
   stretch   (vibrate)

6. What word describes a dog that has a loud, low bark?
   (big)   small

Unit E • Chapter 2   (page 1 of 4)   Assessment Guide AG 77

---

7. Which bell makes a higher sound?
   (small bell)   big bell

8. A whistle makes a sound with a high pitch. How fast do its parts vibrate?
   (fast)   slow

9. Which one often makes a softer sound?
   (kitten)   cat

10. Which makes a louder sound?
    (shout)   whisper

11. Draw a musical instrument you pluck to make a sound. stringed instrument

AG 78 Assessment Guide   (page 2 of 4)   Unit E • Chapter 2

Name _____

12. Draw a musical instrument you beat to make sound. drum

Part III Process Skills Application 6 points each

Process skills: investigate, use numbers, form a hypothesis
Write the letter that best describes the amount of water in each bottle.

13. _A_
14. _C_
15. _B_

A. about $\frac{1}{4}$ cup
B. about $\frac{1}{2}$ cup
C. about 1 cup

Unit E • Chapter 2   (page 3 of 4)   Assessment Guide AG 79

Name _____

16. Circle the letter for the bottle that makes the highest sound when you blow across its top.
    A   B   (C)

17. Draw a small bell. Then draw one that is a little larger and one that is a lot larger.

18. Color the bell that makes the lowest sound.
    The largest bell should be colored.

AG 80 Assessment Guide   (page 4 of 4)   Unit E • Chapter 2

Answer Key

AG 117 Assessment Guide

Unit E

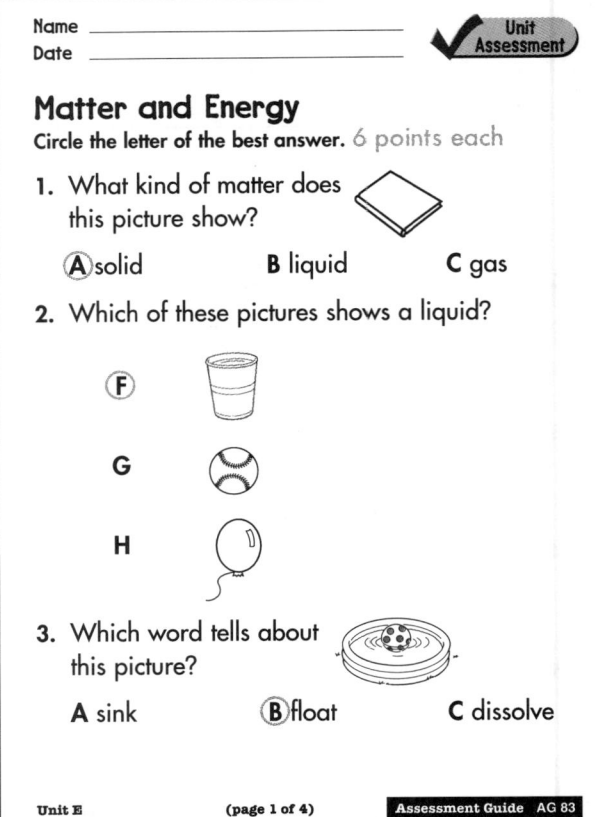

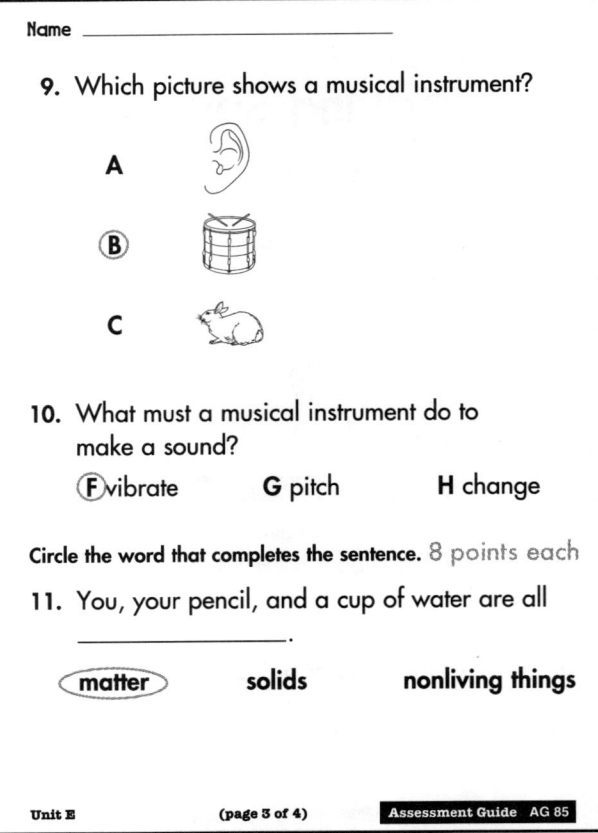

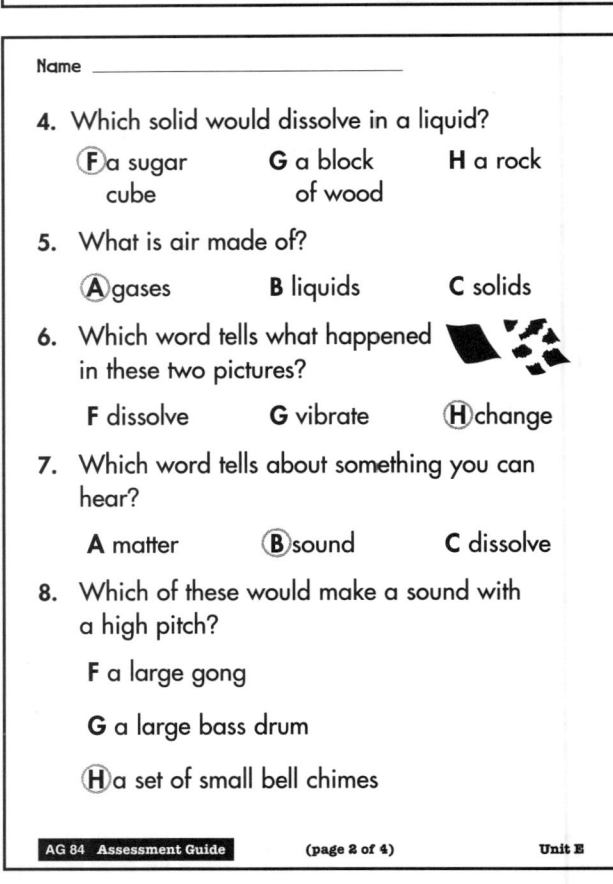

AG 118 Assessment Guide

Answer Key

Unit F • Chapter 1

Name _____
Date _____

Chapter Assessment

Pushes and Pulls

Part I Vocabulary 5 points each

Draw a line to match each word with its picture.

1. push
2. pull
3. curve
4. wheel
5. speed

Circle the word that completes the sentence.

6. A push or a pull is a

   surface   (force)   block

---

7. Moving from one place to another is called

   (motion)   ramp   smooth

8. The top or outside of something is called its

   friction   push   (surface)

9. A force that makes it harder to move things is

   pull   speed   (friction)

Part II Science Concepts and Understanding 8 points each

10. Circle the things that are being pushed.

Name _____

11. Put an X under the animal that is moving faster.

    ___   X

Circle the letter of the correct answer.

12. A path that changes directions is a

    A miss   (B) curve   C hit

13. A ball rolls farther on a

    F rough surface
    (G) smooth surface
    H bumpy surface

14. Circle the surface that has more friction.

Name _____

Part III Process Skills Application 15 points

Process skills: measure, draw a conclusion

15. Look at the pictures.
    Then complete the chart.

    Meters Moved in One Minute

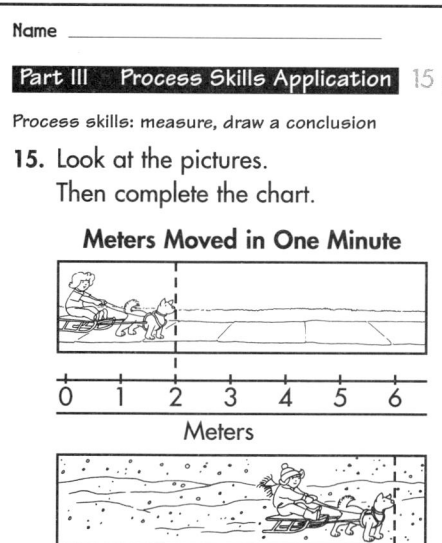

    Meters Moved in One Minute

On the sidewalk	2 meters
On the snow	6 meters

Answer Key

Unit F • Chapter 2

Magnets

Part I Vocabulary 4 points each

Draw a line from the word to the picture it goes with.

1. poles
2. repel
3. attract

Circle the best answer.

4. A piece of iron that can pull things is a ___.

   rock   stone   (**magnet**)

5. A magnet's ___ is how strongly it pulls.

   pole   (**strength**)   plan

6. A ___ can pass through paper.

   (**magnetic force**)   natural force   small force

---

7. A magnet can ___ the things it attracts.

   (**magnetize**)   repel   push

Part II Science Concepts and Understanding

8. Circle things a magnet attracts. 6 points each

   (nail and car circled)

9. Which pole will attract the S pole of another magnet? Put an **X** on it.

   [S | **X**]

10. Put an **X** on the pole that will repel the S pole of another magnet.

    [**X** | N]

---

11. Write the word that completes *both* sentences.

    All magnets have ___ in them.

    Magnets attract objects that are made of ___.   **iron**

Write the letter of the best answer.

A 12. Where is a magnet's pull the strongest?
   A at the poles
   B in the middle
   C above the magnet

H 13. What can you make a magnet from?
   F a crayon
   G a book
   H a paper clip

B 14. What kind of magnet is found in the ground?
   A a gem stone
   B a lodestone
   C a diamond

Part III Process Skills Application 15 points each

Process skills: infer, investigate

15. Put an **X** by the sentence that tells what you can infer from this picture.

    ___ The nail repels the paper clip.

    X The nail has been magnetized.

16. You plan to investigate whether you can make a magnet out of a nail. Write **1**, **2**, and **3** to show the order of the steps you would take.

    1 See if the nail will pull paper clips.

    3 Touch the nail to the paper clips again to see if it will pull them.

    2 Stroke the nail with a magnet ten times in the same direction.

AG 120 Assessment Guide   **Answer Key**

Unit F

Forces

Circle the letter of the best answer. 6 points each

1. Which word tells about a kind of a force?
   - A straight
   - (B) push
   - C surface

2. Which is a change in direction?
   - F up and down
   - (G) curve
   - H friction

3. Which of these words tells a way things can move?
   - (A) straight
   - B friction
   - C magnet

4. Which word tells how an object moves from one place to another?
   - F poles
   - G surface
   - (H) motion

5. Which of these surfaces has the least amount of friction?
   - A wood
   - B carpet
   - (C) ice

6. Which word tells about this picture?
   - F force
   - (G) wheel
   - H push

7. What do all magnets attract?
   - A motion
   - (B) iron
   - C friction

8. Which magnet has the most strength?

   (F)

   G

   H

9. Which picture shows two magnets that will repel each other?
   - A [N S] [N S]
   - B [S N] [S N]
   - (C) [N S] [S N]

10. Which one of these can you magnetize?
    - F a glass of water
    - (G) an iron nail
    - H a wooden wheel

Circle the word that completes the sentence. 8 points each

11. How quickly something moves is called its _____.
    - friction
    - push
    - (speed)

12. Magnetic _____ can pull through paper.
    - motion
    - (force)
    - friction

13. A magnetic force is strongest when two magnets are _____.
    - (close together)
    - far apart
    - in a liquid

Write the answer in the blank. 8 points each

14. A force is a push or a __pull__.

15. The two places on a magnet where the pulling force is the greatest are called the __poles__.

Answer Key